MACCI MAGIC

Extracting Greatness From Yourself and Others

MACCI MAGIC

Extracting Greatness From Yourself and Others

Rick Macci
with Jim Martz

Foreword by Andy Roddick

New Chapter Press

Macci Magic! is published by New Chapter Press (www.NewChapterMedia.com) and is distributed by the Independent Publishers Group (www.IPGBook.com).

Printed in Canada

The cover photo is courtesy of the author. The internal photos are courtesy of Art Seitz, except for the Andy Roddick photo, which is courtesy of the Maureen Connolly Brinker Tennis Foundation (www.mcbtennis.org)

For more information on this title or New Chapter Press contact:

Randy Walker
Managing Partner
New Chapter Press
1175 York Ave
Suite #3s
New York, NY 10065
Rwalker@NewChapterMedia.com

Contents

INTRODUCTION

Rick Macci is considered the top developmental tennis coach in the world. His body of work over the past 30 years has become legendary.

He is a United States Professional Tennis Association (USPTA) Master Professional and is enshrined in the USPTA Florida Hall of Fame in addition to the Hall of Fame of his hometown of Greenville, Ohio for both tennis and basketball. Rick has been USPTA Florida Division Coach of the Year seven times and recipient of the 2003 Alex Gordon Award for USPTA Professional of the Year in North America. He is also an instructional editor for *Tennis* magazine.

Rick's amazing motivational skills and a unique ability to deliver the message with an uncanny communication menu have made him one of the most in-demand clinicians and keynote speakers in the world for any venue. He has appeared on all major U.S. television networks and is a featured instructor in the award-winning videos "On Court with USPTA" for many years on the Tennis Channel.

Rick has been the personal coach of five players who have been ranked No. 1 n the world: Venus and Serena Williams, Andy Roddick, Jennifer Capriati and Maria Sharapova. He has been a consultant for Donald Trump Management and serves on the USPTA Player Development board.

His tennis academy in Boca Raton, Florida has produced students who have won more than 132 United States Tennis Association national titles and all four junior Grand Slam tournaments. To this day, Rick teaches more than 50 hours a week to players age 4 to touring pros and also consults for the USTA's national Player Development program.

He has also created a teaching methodology with sports science guru Dr. Brian Gordon and his academy offers cutting edge 3D analysis of stroke mechanics with an actual MRI of players' strokes. It's considered the premier teaching tool in the world.

ACKNOWLEDGMENTS

Whenever you write a book there are many people to thank. First off, I don't have enough space to thank everybody that I know I'm going to forget. So, if I don't have you on the next few pages and you think you should have or could have been mentioned, I want you to know I really did 100 percent think of you and want to thank you right here and now before you get more upset that I didn't mention your name!

Now that I covered that base, first off I want to thank my dad, who passed away when I was 12 years old. Even though I don't remember a lot, I do remember he got me into several sports and that really laid the cornerstone for me and my wiring. Next my mom, whom I tell always she is the best mom I ever had! She is No. 1 and everybody else, sorry to say, is a distant second. But please keep trying!

I want to thank my three beautiful daughters, Lisa, Farrah and Ginger, for understanding their dad and the crazy, and I mean crazy, hours I work. I would write more about them but I'm working!

Next my super human one-of-a-kind step dad Jack for being one step ahead (get it?) and for your words of wisdom and for care of my mom all these years. You're an incredible person at age 92 to still play 27 holes of golf a day and most of all drink four Bud Lites! That alone is very impressive! That is definitely world class!

To my sister Toni for making me a great competitor at a young age and always, and I mean always, fighting with me when we were kids. Just kidding! Relax!!! To her super husband Ken, for leaving me alone and never visiting me in Florida. Thank you so much and keep up the good job! Just kidding again. Relax. See you soon.

To my special angel Maria for always telling me what I don't want to hear but need to hear. But it's OK to mix it up a little more!

To my awesome niece Kelli for letting me babysit you when you were growing. That in-depth experience in babysitting for kids and some parents has served me well in the tennis world!

To Ray and Joanne Lear, my uncle and aunt, for being a big influence on me when I was growing up. Please still keep influencing as it is a work in progress. To their sons Randy and Rob Lear for building my confidence as kids by me beating you on a regular basis, and I mean regular basis, in every sport.

To Ned and Cheryl Denlinger, my uncle and aunt, for letting me stay with you in Dayton, Ohio, when I was younger and finding my way. And I'm so so glad I found my way out of your house real quick! Also to my now late great uncle Steve Swank, for making me play football against you every Thanksgiving in the below freezing Greenville arctic temperatures when I was a kid, as maybe deep down inside that is why I really wanted to be in Florida and be in the sun all day. I'm still thawing out!!!

To the late Tim Heckler, former CEO of the United States Professional Tennis Association. Words cannot ever explain how I felt about Tim and what he has done for me, so I will say no words.

To the Hisham Abaza family for being the most loyal, dedicated family of 10 years and still going strong and raising two unreal polite, considerate and appreciative kids in Jan and Marwan. You 100 percent understood there was more that students could learn from me than the game of tennis. You taught your kids the grass is not greener elsewhere. It is usually more slippery but you're still the one and only who has to mow it!

To Marc and Michelle Price. Your friendship has been priceless! Ha!! I knew at age 4, during Gabriella's first lesson and she fired a supersonic all-in aggressive 50-mile-an-hour forehand and almost took my head off, she could be one of the best in the country or get into a lot of trouble!!! By the way, since you're a chiropractor, my neck ... it still tweaked from ducking! We will talk!

To one of my best friends ever, Dr. Brian Gordon, a true pioneer in the field of biomechanics. Thank you Brian for sharing your genius with me and extracting more greatness out of me, and you didn't even have to use your 3D cameras on my brain!

Special thanks to the Boca Lago Country Club and its members for giving me the arena to do my thing and treating me like family. Now that I think about it, you don't have to treat me like family!

To the incredible Jim Martz, a long-time friend, just a great guy for putting up with me changing every page. If you're reading this now I promise there are no more changes! Your patience is a gift, and eyesight is even better to read my writing!

To a world-class player and more importantly a world-class person Andy Roddick. Thanks Andy for a great foreword. You would have beaten Federer, Rafa and Joker more if you would have moved forward more into the court! Thanks to a great father Richard Williams for teaching me not to really trust anybody, anytime, anywhere! Trust me on that one! To Stefano Capriati, Jennifer's dad, for serving great pasta at Grenelefe, much better than your own serve! To Yuri Sharapova, Maria's dad, for listening to me and not changing Maria to a lefty at age 11. I told you no way a million times don't change her to a lefty! And, see, you got millions the right way! To Rong Dad and Grace Ho, Tommy's parents, for bringing your son to me at age 9. It was an amazing journey but sometimes a tough road to ho ... ho!!!

I also need to thank my No. 1 student of all time. He is always calm and always on his toes. He is very quick, has unreal agility and balance, stays low to the ground, takes short little steps and has a nice vertical jump. He gets massages frequently, sleeps eight hours a night and is very, very coachable and has a great attitude, and never complains. I hope my cat Buddy enjoys this book. See, I love to teach! Even animals! Meow!

And most of all I want to thank me for being me and pushing me to become me. Thank you so much, me, for extracting greatness from me and keep up the good work on me! Signed me!

-Rick Macci
Boca Raton, Fla.
2013

FOREWORD – Andy Roddick

When I think about Rick Macci and the time I spent as a young pupil of his in the mid 1990s, a thousand great memories of my tennis childhood come back to me. Flag football and private lessons, summer camps and Rick giving me a chance to play with the older kids if he felt I had "earned it." I think about my first memories of my dear lifelong friends Venus and Serena Williams and thoughts of a bunch of other players and wondering where they all ended up and what they might be doing.

To this day if people ask me who is the best tennis teacher in the world for a young kid, I would say Rick's name immediately. I remember his enthusiasm for teaching me the game, and frankly, making me feel very special as a kid. As I think about it, he's also one of the very few who helped me along the way, who never wanted anything from me when I became successful. I know he loved teaching. Whenever Rick was on the court, he was at his happiest.

I always wonder if Rick had been more of a big self promoter like other coaches in America, how big his legacy would be in the grand scheme of coaches in this country and around the world. I confidently assume he would be at the top. Self promotion was never his game. Rick is not only a world-class coach but a teacher of the game of tennis. I think about Rick from time to time, and I always hope he is happy and content. I genuinely care because I feel like he was such a big part of giving me the life that I am lucky to have now. Every kid should be as lucky as I was to have a GREAT teacher in whatever sport or activity they are into.

I hope that you enjoy this book and get to experience part of the "Macci Magic" that I was fortunate to benefit from first hand.

PREFACE – Thomas Ho

The ability to recognize and give credit to individuals that have been influential in one's life does not necessarily come with time. It's a culmination of experiences that allows an individual to reflect objectively and openly which typically leads to a realization that their success was not achieved alone. At a young age, the foundation of who we become is shaped and defined by the decisions we make, the challenges we face and most importantly, the individuals that choose to influence our lives. It would be impossible to reminisce on my childhood without mentioning Rick Macci. However, my perspective and insight of Rick's influence on my life is quite different today versus what it would have been if I were writing this fifteen years ago when I retired from the tour. Since my retirement, I earned a GED and an undergraduate degree, obtained my first corporate job, became a husband, and am a father of two beautiful children (Braeden, 11, and McHaley, 9). It is with this perspective I reflect on what Rick Macci has and will always mean to me.

I was an average junior player with a passion for the game, living in a small town in central Florida. Rick was a Director of Tennis at a resort not too far from where I lived, surrounded by ten miles of orange groves. How we found each other can only be described as fate. How was it possible Rick could one day become one of the greatest teaching professionals in the world? It was clear he possessed several qualities inherent in every world-class professional, regardless of their respective field. Rick had a burning desire to be the best. He was a true student of the game. Rick was a voracious reader and watched tennis constantly. He pushed himself to identify or create the next evolution of the game. I can remember how fixated and focused he was on implementing the psychological side. He preached visualization on and off the court. Rick had me imagine hitting the perfect strokes every night before I went to bed. However, in my opinion, the greatest quality Rick possessed was his ability to connect with me and what he was willing to do to help me maximize my full potential. Where I saw a shy, timid, unconfident kid, Rick saw raw talent in a coachable student. His dedication, positive motivation, high energy and belief that I could accomplish anything I put my mind to started activating the dormant strengths within me that would be the foundation of who I am today. Rick focused on my mental side early on. He wrote well over a thousand motivational letters to me, sometimes two or three a day. Each day the boundaries of my imagination, but more importantly my expectations of how good I should be, started to broaden and grow. As far as physical athleticism went, well this was a little more challenging! Unfortunately, I did not have a 40-inch vertical and was no Usain Bolt. However, Rick was relentless in his effort and approach to maximize my physical abilities. Rick enrolled me in boxing and Tae Kwon Do to improve my footwork and flexibility. I wore ankle weights to school to strengthen my legs. In fact, I remember laying in bed reading a book during a tournament when all of sudden my book went flying across the room and a jump rope appeared out of nowhere! It was impossible for me not to be engulfed by Rick's intensity, passion, dedication and desire to be the best. Looking back, this was clearly Macci's Magic!

1

WIRING AND INSPIRING

I think whenever you have success, there's always a story within a story. My upbringing and where I came from was a very, very unique situation. I grew up in Greenville, Ohio, a small but amazing town of about 10,000 people in southwestern Ohio. You name it, for kids, Greenville had it. We lived in the city park with baseball diamonds, tennis courts, basketball courts, football fields, a track, horseshoe area, bandstand, shelter houses for picnics, pools, ponds and a huge playground. It was just an unbelievable town, very unique and kid friendly with beauty everywhere. It's one of the most incredible environments for kids and family anywhere in the United States. And you can take that to the bank.

When I was younger, and because my parents were golfers and were very good golfers (county champions), our family was always at the Greenville Country Club. So growing up I pretty much had a golf club in my hand and I got very good very quickly. Probably by age 10, I was shooting around 84 for 18 holes. Some people used to call me the "The Arrow" because I could hit it straight every time. I hit it straighter at age 10 than I do now. Is that crazy or what? Now I'm the sparrow instead of the arrow. I guess experience is overrated. I'd play morning, noon and night. I'd play 36 holes. I played golf all the time!!

Back then I just always did everything with a ball, whether baseball, hockey, football, basketball, golf. My mom said it was always me with a ball. And as time went on, when I was around 12, my dad passed away and it seemed pretty much after that we never really played at the country club anymore and golf wasn't really a big thing that I did.

Since we lived in the park, and when I say the park, there were a lot of houses around. We lived very close to the tennis courts, probably within a quarter of a mile. When I was around 13 years old, I would go down there, with my used wood Davis tennis racquet in hand, and play. I just somehow gravitated toward tennis. I hit the ball seemingly 24 hours a day, seven days a week against the backboard. There were six tennis courts -- the nets were all steel and the courts were chipped up -- and there would always be some guys around playing. I always played on court No. 1 and I would write my name with a piece of chalk or a rock on the court: "This is Rick Macci's court!" I did this a lot, especially if the rain washed it away. I was born in 1954, so this was the mid-60's. Tennis really hadn't taken off as it did in the 1970s. I think a lot of people back then who played tennis had no idea they were going to be in the forefront of the incredible tennis boom.

I really enjoyed hitting the ball against the backboard, but I also enjoyed playing other sports. I was I was an all-star pitcher in baseball, and in football I'd win the Punt, Pass and Kick almost every year. I was also very good in hockey. The ponds would freeze in Greenville and everybody would go skating on the ponds every night and we'd play hockey. I could handle the puck like a wizard and I was as fast as lightning. I just had very good hand-eye coordination and skills. I just always loved to compete and loved to be around competition and anything to do with a ball or some type of object. It seemed like it was always part of my DNA. I loved sports and loved to compete. I just love to battle, keep score, win or lose. I hated to lose more than I loved to win. I'd create games and situations in my young mind and instill pressure. I really loved pressure and the moment. I really think being creative and picturing things in my mind really helped me for the future in other sports and situations when it was crunch time.

I also was always the first one on the tennis courts, first one on the pond, first one on the basketball court, first one on the football field. At least I was first in something! If you're early, ready and you're prepared, you're already prepared early.

I just hated to lose, but losing made me more determined. I also always dreamed a lot. I visualized a lot. I pictured a lot of things in my mind before I would do it. I was a very creative kid and I had a lot of energy and motivation and just loved the bright lights. Why? I'm not sure. I think when you love doing something you do whatever you can to be the best you can be and you just add layers of the big time to make it more exciting.

One big part of my wiring was that I was always the organizer. I'd be the one who called everybody to make sure there was going to be 12 guys to play hockey. I'd be the guy to make sure there were 16 guys to play football or to make sure we had 10 guys to play basketball at the park that day or a gym in town. And I had a list with everybody's phone number and I'd call them and check it off. This was a regularly structured routine that I did to make it happen like clockwork. This is pretty interesting stuff for somebody 12 or 13 to organize things and glue everything together. I always had tremendous motivation to do this with all the games we played. A lot of my buddies growing up are still mad at me for waking them up at 7 a.m. on a Saturday!

And that's key to kind of where I am today and how I'm wired because I think, for whatever reason, those leadership qualities to bring people together, to inspire people and just be a leader and to show people, really started at a young age. Whether it went into tennis or another form of business, who would know? But I think everybody can recall some of those things that maybe influenced them in their lives. Since many people around the world have interviewed me and they've asked me, "You didn't lose in the final of Wimbledon or you didn't do this, how did you kind of end up being one of the world's best coaches?" I always go back to the beginning. I think those qualities have played a big part of what I ended up doing and where I am today.

As time went on in my childhood I started hitting more tennis balls, especially in the summer. I loved it and I wanted to play all the time. I thought it was the biggest treat in the world to go with some of the older guys who would drive me over to nearby towns like Troy or Piqua, Ohio, where they actually had cotton nets and they had a court that had regular Laykold surface on it. I felt I landed in the Emerald City! The courts I grew up on kind of looked like courts out of a war-torn area! It looked like they had bomb craters or bullet holes! The courts in Troy and Piqua were regular courts – even with wind screens and new nets. It was so motivating to play there.

The fact that maybe I had very little growing up – and that I had to do things the hard way – is a big part of how I ended up coaching and teaching to this day. This is a major factor in how I see everything differently from every possible angle and I can relate to all ages and levels and take the exact temperature for that player on that day.

I really got hooked on tennis as a kid and my goal was to be the No. 1 player in Greenville, Ohio. And, within a short time, that happened. Not that there was a star-studded cast of players in my town, although there were players that were much older than me when I was 13 or 14, but that was my goal and I achieved it. I also wanted to win the Darke County Championships, which included a bunch of small towns. That was my goal and I was going to play morning, noon and night to do that. I would not be denied. And I ended up winning my age group every year and in the men's division. I always set goals and I always wrote them down. Always.

Anything I could read regarding tennis, whether it would be any type of magazine or newspaper article or book. I would study morning, noon and night. I was such a student of trying to learn and teach myself. I guess a true winner finds a way. I would watch other players that were coming up and observe and study how they hit the ball, how they set up, how they took the racquet back, what type of strategy they used because we couldn't afford lessons. And as scary as it's going to sound to a lot of people, I've never had a lesson in my life. And to this day, I give more lessons than anybody in the United States. You go from one extreme to the other. That is amazing…or is it really?

When I was in high school -- and because I loved to play tennis so much, and because in Ohio it's pretty cold -- many, many times at the end of basketball practice I would run two blocks and go home, eat dinner, and come back to school with my mom in her car and hit tennis balls in front of the car with the lights on bright, shining magnificently on the back of the high school gymnasium building. Sometimes I have to take out a shovel from the trunk and shovel out about a 40-foot long path about the width of the doubles alley, or maybe a little bit more. I'd pull out my all-weather steel T-2000 tennis racquet and I'd start smacking groundstrokes with earmuffs on and a hat for an hour straight. If I didn't laser in and really focus on moving my feet and setting up correctly the ball would come off the wall and end up in the snow drift instead of the runway I cleared for me to practice on. I would just keep ripping groundstrokes for an hour straight because it was all about the repetition, because we really couldn't afford to drive 40 miles to an indoor club in Dayton. To pay money to play tennis in the middle of November, December, January, are you kidding me? Also at the end of basketball practice if there wasn't anything going on in the gym afterwards I would bring my racquet and hit groundstrokes and serves against the wall. People don't realize "Wally" is still undefeated because he always brings it back. If you think about it, Wally is the most rock-solid opponent you'll every play against.

Everybody thought I was crazy (but crazy is good if channeled correctly). I needed to stay dialed in and get the reps! I practiced more than anybody, especially in the summer time. I'll put my practice time up there against anybody that's ever picked up a tennis racquet. Anybody! And I'll tell you why. I'd be out there at 8 a.m., and even if there was no one to play, I'd practice serves. Even in the pouring rain. I just loved to hit the ball. Not liked, but loved it! Even to this day I can hit a serve on a dime and the kids are amazed. A lot of people just think that I'm a coach that taught a lot of great players. They don't realize that I did play and I was very, very good. Like anything in life, getting quality repetition in your sport or craft is the foundation that translates into bigger and better things. It's like shooting a jump shot or foul shot in basketball. The best of the best launch 500 a day, even on their day off, so they never have an off day!

I would hit so many serves, it was amazing. And if no one was there I'd hit against the backboard. It didn't matter what age or level, I just wanted to hit the ball. I'd be out there 8 a.m. to noon and then I'd run home to get a peanut butter and jelly sandwich, some chocolate milk and some Fritos and the I'd come back at 1 o'clock and I'd go until 5 p.m. Then I'd go home and eat a minute steak, a baked potato, salad and some lemonade and go back out to the courts from 6 to 9 p.m. And this was all summer long – for three months. I wouldn't miss a day. I couldn't miss a day!

What happened was, because this Macci guy was getting so good at tennis, he'd always play on the first court. All my friends would hang out at the park courts. There were kids of all ages, all levels and mostly jocks. The football stadium and the school were right next to the courts, so there were hundreds of kids hanging out in the area. However, one focal point was this Macci guy playing on the No. 1 tennis court. It was really a hub where everybody would meet, even guys that played other sports and couldn't even play tennis. They'd get a racquet, or steal my racquet and balls, and they'd be out there trying to play. Talk about Comedy Central!

But it seemed like through my success in high school and branching out, it was like the whole concept of tennis in the town of Greenville took on a life of its own. And I didn't think much about it at the time. When you're a kid growing up, everything looks so big around you but I just loved to compete and have fun.

Now that I look back at the culture that I created there in Greenville, it allowed for them to get even better facilities. We ended up getting all the courts resurfaced and getting all new nets. We got wind screens for the first time ever and they put in three new courts. We went from six courts to nine courts. A lot of this was because it went from a handful of people playing in the town to hundreds. You couldn't even get a court, especially at night. That's just the power you can have over people and things by some success, media attention and being a role model.

Maybe because I didn't really have a role model or someone who helped me pretty much learn how to do things, it was a positive-negative. I think the positive was that I had to figure it out on my own and I was always open to learning. I wasn't structured in a laser-type here's-what-you're-supposed-to-do mentality. On the flip side, as I started getting real good and as I started to become the best player in Greenville, I wanted to become the best player in the

Dayton area and one of the best high school players in the state, and the best player in the Ohio Valley. And then, I entered qualifying of some pro tournaments. The window or ceiling that I had because I was self taught was going to pretty much tap out at 300, 400, 500 in the world. But from not being taught, it was a big leap because I never had that opportunity. But the most important thing, I made the opportunity!

If I had received quality lessons and top-notch training, I would have been a much better player. My development would have been expedited. But I wouldn't trade the other qualities that I had to learn on my own for anything in the world.

I can remember as a kid seeing someone walk up with four racquets and they were all dressed in white. I was down 3-0 before we started the match because I had one T-2000 and that cost $25 and then I had on a T-shirt and some basic shorts. But I could run and I could stop and I could compete and had heart like no other!

But still there's that mental part, handling pressure and delivering. You've just got to go through those things before you grow mentally and figure it out. On the flip side, as I said, I wouldn't trade it for anything because I did so much hockey, football and basketball that my footwork on the tennis court was like popcorn popping in the microwave -- and with extra butter. Everybody was kind of blown away by my movement on the tennis court. And it's a great lesson for any kid, parent or coach. It was all naturally developed from other sports.

It's not just speed or quickness but the adjustment steps around the ball, how my feet moved, and the best thing is that no one taught me how to move. Like I said, the movement of other sports really enhanced my footwork for tennis. It was more the other things that dovetailed into being a great mover on the tennis court, not just the genetics or maybe, oh, he had some quickness and some speed. It was more the specific footwork, because playing basketball helped me. (I was inducted into the hall of fame for my high school for basketball and tennis.) When you play defense in basketball, it's almost identical to a great mover in tennis. You're low, you're shuffling your feet, you're on your toes. You're changing direction, you're starting, you're stopping, you're going up and going back and you're always bouncing. I played point guard and I loved to trick people, I loved to set people up. I always wanted to help others and be the assist guy and it kind of goes with the way I teach today. I'm very much into helping others, I'd rather have others get more than me. I get benefit out of seeing others achieve and have success.

You can go all the way back to when I was a point guard in basketball. I saw the court differently, I saw it before it happened. I could just feel it. Occasionally I wanted the ball in my hands when the game was on the line, like the time I made an off-balance 17-foot shot as the buzzer screamed for a 54-53 overtime victory.

Wired and inspired as a kid

The Dayton Daily News ran a photo of teammates, cheerleaders and fans piling on me and the caption said: "Somewhere in that mob is Rick Macci after game-winning shot." I practiced that shot thousands of times in my driveway as a kid ... 3...2...1...Macci at the buzzer ... Nothing but net!!! And thousands of times in my head I pictured it, saw it and made it real with the fans in the stands. Being there mentally so many times and wanting the ball, wanting the pressure and more importantly expecting to make it, not hoping to make it, is the reason why I ended up at the bottom of that pile!!! The feeling of helping others and being the assist guy continued through the 1970s, '80s, '90s and even today. In basketball at age 21 or 22, everybody thought I played Division I as a point guard because I analyzed and saw things differently. My senior year in high school, I had multiple scholarship offers to play basketball and tennis. I loved to play basketball but my biggest concern was I'd much rather read *Tennis* magazine than *Basketball Weekly*. I'd much rather keep playing tennis. One time playing in a basketball game I broke my left wrist when a guy undercut me. It turned out to be the greatest thing that happened to my tennis career! Growing up I always had a two-handed backhand groundstroke and volley, and because I had a cast on my left arm, I had to use my right hand only to slice. From this situation, I would still play tennis every day and I still played tournaments with a cast on my hand. It helped my backhand slice and my backhand volley because I volleyed with two hands. Tossing on the serve was very interesting since I had a cast on my left wrist. But at least I kept my arm straight!

What was really amazing was that my forehand improved more than ever before because I didn't want to hit a backhand because all I could do was slice it. I'd run around it as much as possible. My footwork also improved dramatically because I was running around my backhand slice. My footwork became more rhythmic.

I improved more in those three months than I did in my whole life! And I spent more time visualizing my shots because I had to make up ground so I didn't lose ground, so I worked harder mentally to picture things in my mind. I didn't lose a beat. Once I got the cast off, my two-handed backhand was back intact but I had a more well-rounded, complete game. So I guess every year I should send that guy who undercut me in the basketball game a Christmas card. He helped my tennis game more than anybody I've ever been around. And he wasn't even a coach. To tell you the truth, he was more of a jerk. So, see what I mean? You can take a negative and make it into a positive.

I didn't want to leave Greenville. I loved Greenville but I just didn't want to go to an Ohio State or another college far away. I took some classes at Wright State University, a small school in Dayton. I was too good for the team. I could beat everybody 0 and 0. I was ready to make that next leap. I could play with college All-Americans and I could beat them.

I was at that level by the time I was 20, so I started working at an indoor club in Troy, Ohio. Tom Frydell, the man who hired me, was the director of tennis there. He was friends with such tennis legends as Don Budge, Bill Tilden, Ellsworth Vines and Jack Kramer. He had been around the block and had some of the most prestigious jobs in the world. Tom was in his 70s and he said, "Rick you're a very good player and have a super personality and you're going to do incredibly well teaching tennis."

So I went there and started teaching and didn't know that much about teaching. And once I started really helping people, after a month he brought me in his office and said, "I don't know exactly where it's going to end up but I feel you could be one of the greatest teachers of all time in the history of tennis." That after only one month of working there! I looked at this guy and I didn't even know what he meant. He said, "The way you are with people, the way you communicate, the way you can describe things, as you keep doing this you'll gain knowledge. You're going to be a special coach."

I didn't even think about it at the time because I was still worried about becoming a good player. I still had maybe some dreams to play on what they now call the Futures circuit – the tennis equivalent to minor-league baseball. I was still playing tennis and basketball every day because I just loved to compete. Back in the day in the Dayton area, they had this circuit called the Dayton Grand Prix. It was put together by Hank Jungle. Hank put together this circuit in Dayton and it was like having my own Futures tournament in my back yard. In no time my nickname was "The Greenville Gunner." The way I hit my groundstrokes eventually I became one of the best players in the area and never even had a lesson! But I had the wiring to compete. I just loved the bright lights and pressure.

While teaching tennis in Troy, Ohio, I was for the first time in my life playing tennis year round and I was becoming rock solid as a player. I really loved to teach. I really loved to help others. The more I taught and saw how kids and adults improved and how I could extract things from inside of them to do more, the more it inspired me. I could teach 10 straight hours and keep getting stronger as the day went on. The passion for teaching kept growing deeper and deeper. I just knew this is what I wanted to do as a career. So I wanted to get my teaching certification from the U.S. Professional Tennis Association. I called a guy who gave the test in Cincinnati named Steve Cantardi, who is now a good friend of mine. I said, "Can I come and watch you teach?" He was blown away because people just don't do that, even though a lot of people today now come to me and ask that. He said he had a lesson Saturday morning. I got my mom's car and drove the 65 miles to Cincinnati from Greenville and sat there, with a notebook, and watched this guy teach.

I didn't really remember that much of the technical but the one thing that I did notice more than anything was his passion and his motivational skills, which dovetailed right into how Rick Macci was wired. So I thought alright, I might be good at this. I was there for three or four hours and I eventually ended up getting certified through the USPTA. I wanted to become the best that I could become but I knew at the end of the day that I had to eventually go to California or Florida. I just knew that I'd be limited if I stayed in the home town I grew up in. Even though I was working in Troy, Ohio, I just knew I had to get where there is warm weather. I had no aspirations to teach kids or adults, it didn't matter. I'd teach a cat. Meow. I just love teaching and I love helping people, so I just said I need to get a little more of the business experience.

From there I answered an advertisement in Vineland, New Jersey. Someone had an opening for a tennis pro and I called them and they said, "You want to come for an interview?" I said, "Yeah." So I went and talked to these people. It was a small club but I could run the business side, do payroll, do accounting, be the head pro. I said I've got to leave Greenville so I can let go and I can go for this dream of just being the best I can be. I had to follow my dream.

So I went to Vineland, New Jersey and it was a great experience. I learned a lot and became the No. 1 player in New Jersey and, for whatever it's worth, one of the best players in the Middle States. I was still playing at a high level. I was very much into playing, but again it just seemed like standing room only for lessons, just like it was in Troy, even though I didn't have a tenth of the knowledge I have today. I just had a way to communicate with people and analyze things and figure things out. Even if I didn't know why certain things happened, I could figure it out and explain it. That's always been one of the keys of what I've done in teaching.

I was in New Jersey for about a year, and one day I was sitting in my apartment and there was a tournament that came on TV. It was called the United Airlines Sunbird Cup and it was at this place called Grenelefe Golf and Tennis Resort near Haines City, Florida. Martina Navratilova was playing Andrea Jaeger and the announcer said, "There's this new place out in an orange grove and they're going to build condos and they've got a 54-hole golf course and they've got plans for a convention center." I'm thinking this is a unique situation, but I didn't think anything more about it. The following week, I was home and not teaching because it was raining, I didn't have anything to do so I called down to Grenelefe and spoke to someone about tennis teaching positions. The guy told me, "Listen, I have a stack of resumes on my desk I can't even see over. If you want to fly down here, we're going to make a decision in two weeks. If you want to fly down on your nickle fine, but like I said I've got a stack of resumes and we're ready to hire somebody now."

So I figured what the heck, I don't have anything to really do for the weekend, I'll go to Florida. I jumped on an airplane and went down to Orlando. My plane got in late – in the middle of the night. Grenelefe was off the beaten path -- out in the boondocks -- and I'm feeling like I was in another world with all of these creatures called palmetto bugs that were as big as ping pong balls with legs. To make a long story short I was there two days. Not one person played tennis. But it was paradise. The place was beautiful. The tennis village had a 1,700-seat sunken stadium and 13 courts. It was June and the temperature was 103 degrees and humid steam was coming off the courts. There were many frogs in the ready position that never made it off the baseline. Ribbit. There was nobody playing tennis and I was thinking, 'I'm not doing this.' I did all the interview processes and talked to the guy for hours and hours and we even played a few sets. He took me back to the airport after being with me pretty much all day Saturday and Sunday. He said, "If you want the job it's yours."

At the time I was thinking that I was not going to accept the job, but I told him to give me a few days to think about it. So I thought about it and I decided it was an opportunity for me to take the ball and run with it and I could build something, I could do something that has never been done. There was nothing really before me at this place and I love challenges. This challenge would be the biggest ever. My wiring was so ready to make Grenelefe Resort a household name and for it to go over the rainbow.

I said, "I'm rolling the dice." I ended up taking a pay cut but said, "I'm coming." I was there all summer and I taught five hours of lessons in three months. Then I was thinking this is the worst mistake I made in my life, but my golf game improved and my sun tan was world class!

But I looked at it as a challenge, a positive not a negative. It was going to be special and internationally known if I made it happen. Where it got interesting is the fact that they had no local base. There was no membership. People would come down to visit as a vacation destination. But they're building a convention center and there were going to be corporate tournaments. I could create and put together my own little dog and pony show with these corporate tournaments. Instead of saying, "Fred you're playing with Bill and Bob and Jack and you're on court six, go over there," I had an opportunity to really do something that's never been done. I put together this corporate round robin presentation. I knew we were going to do a lot of these. I looked at it like I was competing against Innisbrook or Saddlebrook or any resort in the United States. I loved to compete. The competitiveness is 'I'm competing against them and myself.' It was my wiring expecting to do my very best. I not only had to think out of the box but I had to build the box to extract more greatness from within. I wanted to do it differently than the Boca Raton Resort & Club. I wanted to do it differently than any of these resorts in the U.S., period.

I wondered how I could make these corporate round robins different than others. So as soon as the guests came off the trolley, say 60 guys from IBM, they'd start walking to the tennis complex and I had the Olympic theme playing over the P.A. system and you could hear it for miles. Even to the point where the golfers would call up the G.M. and say "What's going on here?" It didn't matter.

These guys have their convention somewhere every year and this year it's Grenelefe's turn. The big ticket item is golf. There'd probably be 200 golfers and 60 tennis players -- that's the way it is. But I wanted to serve the clients better than anyone. So they get off the trolley and these weekend warrior players start to hear the Olympic music and they think, "What the heck?" I'm looking and they're all laughing. Some of these guys are jumping up and down. I've already got their attention. So already compared to everybody else in the United States, they're saying, "This is different. Nothing else. Funnier." Now they come up to this amazing scoreboard and I'm there with my assistant and two girls from the pro shop. We check everybody in, I had this round robin board designed and it was an overview of the tennis complex.

The board was about five feet by about seven feet and was made of plexiglass. I had a map of the tennis complex with all of the courts on it. In front of this plexiglass board I had a hurricane shutter with the Grenelefe logo on it. There were four players assigned to a court, so instead of me giving out pieces of paper and telling people their respective court assignments, I used this board, that actually cost us about $5,000. I would kick things off by saying something like, "First off, I'd like to welcome everybody to Grenelefe Golf and Tennis Resort. I'm Rick Macci, director of tennis, I'd like to introduce you to…. blah, blah, the assistants, whatever. We're going to be doing a round robin presentation for today. Everybody is going to get a different partner each round. We'll do five rounds and the winning team is going to go to center court and we'll do the finals. And after each round I want you to check the board to see where you're going to go to."

I'd put my hand behind my back and press a button and the theme from "Rocky" would play and this hurricane shutter would be going up. Now you've got 60 guys from IBM who've already been hit with a left hook coming off the trolley, now they see this incredible first-class presentation, the theatrics are like Disney World. This thing's coming up in the air, the theme from "Rocky" is playing, they didn't know how it went up in the air, it came right after my last word. And all these guys are CEOs, CFOs, all six- to seven-figure guys, executives, and they're already blown away and I've got every one of them in awe! They're already thinking no matter what happens, Grenelefe is the best. And you know what? We hadn't even started yet.

These guys have round robins at their local club and other places and I can tell by their faces they are super impressed. So I say, "Check the board, it tells who your partner is, who your opponent is and which court you're going to. Leave the can of balls on the court. After you play, come back check the board."

So they go off and play. The next round is put up and the players come back and report their score. They come staggering in and the next round is already up, already organized. So we do that for five rounds. Then one guy has 25 points, some guy has 24 and another 23. We put the No. 1 player and the No. 4 player as a team and No. 2 and No. 3 as a team. But when they go out for their last round, we pretty much know who's going to be in the finals. So the last round is over with, I get on the P.A. and say, "Players report to center court for the finals of the $300,000 IBM Tennis Classic" or whatever we called it. All the guys go there with their Bud Light, their Gatorade, whatever, they're all sitting there on the stadium court and the names are on the scoreboard. The logo of CBS Sports is right there too. The title IBM Tennis Classic is there. So they're going to a 1,700-seat stadium, there are 60 guys and their wives and girlfriends (or both) all there watching. They go onto center court to play. I have ball kids and I get into the umpire's chair and say, "Ladies and gentlemen, welcome to the finals of the $1.98 IBM Tennis Classic. On my left, hailing from Cleveland, Ohio, averaging 28 foot faults a game and 11 bad calls, ranked No. 1 in the state of Ohio, please welcome ... " and I say the guy's name. And right then I hit the crowd cheers. So over the P.A. system I have 20,000 people cheering and the guy almost has a heart attack. It is the Super Bowl! I do the same announcement for all four people and it's all tongue in cheek. I just wanted to make them happy. I just wanted to make it the best. We're in the service business.

They played the four-game match and when there's a bad shot I'd say, "That was one of the worst shots in the history of tennis." And I hit the tape recorder hidden behind my back and 10,000 boos would come over the P.A. system. I had all these things I was working from the umpire's chair. At the end of the match, we'd play the song "The Eye of the Tiger" and they'd shake hands. Afterwards, we'd have a big ceremony and I'd present the big check. I would present the worst player award. I would give a horse's ass award that said, "I brought up the rear in the Grenelefe tournament." They would get their photographs taken with names on the board, CBS Sports, and they'd get a photograph. I'd put it in a folder and gave it to them as a memento to take.

They've now had a two-and-a-half-hour round robin tournament with so much sizzle, so much icing that when people left the resort, even if they spent other time playing golf and at meetings, time after time after time, they'd say the highlight of their stay was the round robin tennis tournament by Rick Macci and his staff. We took it to a level where it was a production like no other! Period! It's all about serving the customers. I didn't want to just serve them. I was competing against the world and we had to make it the best.

So what does this all mean? I think it goes to the wiring. I like to help others. I like to do it better. Find a way, keep improving, make it better. I could have said, "You play with him" and let someone else do it. It not only took on a life of its own to the point that I did 80 of these a year. *Tennis* magazine did a story on it. *Convention and Meetings* magazine said, "No one does it better than Grenelefe." The sales and marketing people, whom I never see because tennis is the step-child, are bringing clients down to view the property and saying, "You've got to meet Rick." They just want me to tell them about the tournament. We had people playing tennis, sometimes 20 to 30 people -- and some didn't even play! They just wanted the dog and pony show. And what a show it was! It was definitely show time!

To me that was so fulfilling when I was making others feel good. That is a big part of how I am. When the resort got built out and more people started coming and I put together this tennis grand prix for Central Florida that became the largest grassroots tennis program in the Southeast.

I'd be getting 450 people per tournament – complete with sponsors! It was a Thursday night, Friday, Saturday, Sunday event. We had the P.A. system and we had all sorts of fun. The people in Polk County, Osceola County, Hillsborough County, they had just never seen anything like it. It was an event. Plus free beer. For that alone guys would enter! It was so unique, so special and first class from A to Z. It was the most talked about event in Polk County for eight years. I loved to create and build! Period.

We were also doing about 12 USTA tournaments a year, maybe once in awhile a Satellite or Futures or "minor league" tournament sprinkled in there. But here's where this was all headed: When a doctor named Rong Dad Ho came over from Winter Haven, Florida, and said, "I have three boys." His two older sons were OK players, but in the nine-year-old boy Tommy I saw something different. The way he held the tennis racquet was like nothing I had ever seen. He had a severe western grip. I couldn't tell which side of the racquet he was going to hit the ball with. I asked Leo Katz, who was the USPTA tester in Florida, about it and he said, "I'd change that grip." Even the late, great Australian tennis coach Harry Hopman (Tommy went to a camp of his) said, "You've got to get him to an eastern grip." And I said, "Listen, he has more racquet speed than Rod Laver. I've never seen his contact point shift, ever, it's always in the same place. The way he accelerates is ahead of his time. It's unique. It's a short stroke, the hitting side of the body, like a very aggressive ping pong shot." Here you've got Rick Macci, who's this guy at Grenelefe, and you've got Hopman and guys who write the curriculum for organizations saying change the grip. I said, "I think it's a weapon. What you see is unorthodox. I think there's something special. The art of the deal, when he gets to the contact point he's rock solid! The rhythm is already there. The grip could be a little tougher for return of serves but we can work on that."

This kid became very, very good. He also became like my son and I took him under my wing. I had one goal: I had to be all in and influence his wiring to extract greatness. He was kind of lazy, kind of negative. But I knew I could change that. My goal was simple: This kid was going to be the best in the country. He had the talent but he missed a lot of the inner qualities. I had more time obviously because I didn't have kids of my own. I wasn't married at the time. I was going to do anything to get him to be the best in the country. Period! Two years later, not only was he the best, he won every singles and doubles title in the USTA under 12 competition -- and that had never been done. He also became the youngest ever, at 15 years old, to win the USTA National Championship at Kalamazoo, Michigan – a record that still stands today! Through his success people said, "Maybe this guy Macci knows something." This was never my intention. My intention was to be the best that I could be. So really through Tommy's success, that's what spring-boarded Jennifer Capriati coming to train with me as well as the Williams sisters and everybody else.

It really triggered me saying, "OK, why do all these people want to come? Maybe I need to board them, maybe I need a camp." I had no aspirations of any of that stuff. It was through all Tommy's success and now I guess I'm smart! That is life, but you've got to prove yourself every day and never look back.

If you ask people, they will always say how much I cared and how much I tried to figure it out and how I could communicate it. It really goes all the way back to Greenville, Ohio, when I did all the things but at a different entry level. It's that mindset because you acquire the knowledge as you go along. Nothing beats experience. But to be able to do it and extract greatness out of people is a skill. It starts with trying to find a way, never giving up, keep pushing the button until you find that answer. That is me. That's a mindset. Persistence never loses! It is undefeated!

A lot of people get frustrated and they quit, they make excuses. And I never make excuses. It would always be between me and me, because your toughest test in life is always between you and you. It's what you expect of you and what you're going to settle for. Sometimes it can become a little bit too extreme, but with that approach you keep refining it until you're satisfied. And if you're really good, you're never satisfied, because I'm trying to get better even right now. And I've learned more and more just in the last couple years than I did ever because of that mentality of always wanting to get better. If you're not getting ahead you're getting behind.

When you talk of coaching, it's a slippery slope. I really feel, and many people have told me this (which I agree with), I could have coached an NBA team, an NFL team. I could have coached golf. That's just the way I feel. I can figure things out. I don't quit until I figure it out. I know how to motivate people, yet I don't try to motivate people. It just happens. I know how to communicate with them, especially with youth. And I don't try to communicate with them, it's just over time being able to give analogies and give situations. To inspire people is the greatest gift you can give to anybody, because you're getting them to do something they may not be able to do. Everybody needs a helping hand. I'm not talking about how to hit a forehand or backhand, but to get the feedback over the years where parents have said, "Listen, you really helped my kid go from C's to A's." Or they've been on medication and now they're off it. Or "I really think they clean their bedroom because of you ... Their whole attitude toward their brother is changed." I would say, "Great. Can he now come over and clean my bedroom!"

With Tommy Ho

These are powerful things that echo in the way I teach. I'm not out there giving a sermon or anything like that. It's part of the lingo. It's much bigger than the game of tennis. When you get that feedback, and I'm talking thousands, not a handful of people, even people that are in successes in all walks of their life when they're parents or grandparents, those people come back and tell you how you influenced them in a big-time way. This was my calling, to help others and tennis was just the platform.

Forget the X's and O's in the groundstrokes, it's the other things that I feel most proud of. And to me, when you hear people say there are common threads to the late UCLA basketball coaching legend John Wooden, there are a lot of similarities but that's just the way it kind of happened with me.

It's the way I look at these things and figure things out. Go figure. Ha!

The winning and losing will be a byproduct of the preparation and all these things, because you can't control winning and losing. The game of tennis gives people so much more than just groundstrokes, volleys and things like that. I think that I've been consistent ever since in the way that I motivated myself and taught myself to play and how I got so good, so fast. To me that's probably my greatest accomplishment -- how well I taught myself. Once I started giving that to others and saw how I could get someone to run a little faster, to jump a little higher, or how I could instill confidence in someone not to be afraid, or how I could get someone to believe, and how I could get them to look at something totally different than the way they looked at it, that really expedited the learning curve. It's something that a parent and a lot of people can't do. Not that it's a race to the finish line, but I think that is why I had a lot of good kids do things really fast. Sure, I was lucky. But I had to have something to work with. The Williams sisters are a perfect example. They still would have been great if we hadn't worked together, it just wouldn't have happened as fast, but who really knows how it would have turned out?

It's the same with Jennifer Capriati. She was already great. I could see greatness, I knew it. It happened at 13 and 14 because of Rick Macci, there's no doubt. But she would have been great anyway. Opportunity has to be there. Talent has to be there. All these forces have to kind of meet at the right time to maximize someone's ability. A lot of times it doesn't. Some kids don't have a chance, and they might have more ability and more capabilities, they just don't get the chance. So by me being in the position I'm in, I saw how I was influencing how people thought and talked. And when I'd hear the kids say the things that I say, such as "believing is magic, run for every ball, winners find a way, losers make excuses," when I hear them echoing those things and then kind of using that as an outline or a blueprint for their life, forget tennis. It's huge. It's a game changer. People can make a wrong turn. Maybe my influence can help them get back on track.

So that's what makes me feel good about what I've done with the way I teach. That's why a lot of people really don't know me. They see what they see on TV or what they read or what they see in promotions. You can't judge a book by its cover, good or bad. You've got to get in there and feel it from a lot of different directions, then you come up with your own analysis.

I think the ability to motivate others, to get them to do things they had no idea they could do and believe, to me that has been the staple because that's what I did for myself. But I didn't know I was doing it for myself.

How did this happen? My mom was not overly involved and I really didn't have a father to guide me from the time I was young. Who knows how you get those things? But those core values, those grassroots that were put in me are really the wiring. A lot of people when they have a little success they think they can solve all the problems of the world. They think they're the greatest thing since sliced bread, yet I feel I still have a lot to learn even at this stage in the game. I've always been one to learn, because I tell all the coaches, "A smart coach is a smart coach because he knows he's not that smart." You want to keep learning and growing and adding more to your toolbox because life changes every day, even in the field of tennis it changes every day.

Another key thing is that I always was intrigued to figure things out. I don't want to say obsessed, though I guess I would. Even if I go to the movies I'm always trying at the beginning to figure out how it's going to end. And whoever is with me would get mad because I'd tell them how it's going to end. And I wouldn't give 15 possibilities, I'd say, "Here's how it's going to end." Maybe that's why I went to the movies alone a lot. Ha! But most of the time I was right. I just had a feel!

It's the same if I'm watching a football game or basketball on TV and I'm analyzing what's going on. Thousands of students and parents say I look right through it and I explain it differently than anybody they've ever met. I'm three steps ahead of what's coming next and I can communicate that. I think that's another reason why as a speaker or an on-court clinician I've been fortunate to become one of the most in demand worldwide in the game of tennis. That's what I've been told. But I look at me as just one of the guys. Period.

At the end of the day, I just want to share my knowledge and hope I can help others. Those qualities are really simple things, basic things, of wanting to improve, wanting to help others, caring about others, leading by example. I've also never sat down on a tennis court in 20-some years. I don't allow the kids to sit down. Why? I don't know, maybe because then you've just got to get back up. I just think you lead by example. I don't like to waste time. I'm always on time, never late, first one to work, last one to leave. It is kind of like back at the Greenville days. I was the first guy at the football field way ahead of time and the last one to leave. I was the first guy to practice and the last one to leave.

If I'm going to go anywhere, I'm always packed a week ahead of time. I am just always ready. I just believe if you're ready, you don't have to get ready. So all these things I think really resonated when I was a kid.

Regarding teaching, I was always known to be good with older boy players and pros, then I got to be known as good with girls, then I got to be known as unbelievable with younger kids. It seems like whatever students I had in front of me, I was considered the best with that age because I could feel how to deliver the message with that skill level and age. That is the art of the deal when coaching others. But you get stereotyped a little bit. I thought it was funny because I used to be pegged as the guy who works best with nationally-ranked junior boys. Then when I was with Jennifer, Venus and Serena everybody who had a girl thought, well, he's really a master at working with girls, let's go see him. Then I would be working with nationally ranked girls. Then I decided to teach younger kids, and they go on to be the top juniors in the country in their age group. Now there are hundreds around the world who want the Rick Macci experience from age three to seven. Parents around the world want that type of rock-solid foundation. I just want to help anybody, any time, any day. It is that wiring that helps extract greatness from within. It is between me and me. Period.

It could be an adult. I would put the same effort into an 85-year-old man if I was teaching him. It doesn't matter, teaching is teaching. Another thing, all that matters to me is who's on the other side of the net. I've had that ability to focus and just laser into things. I can laser right into what I'm doing and a bomb could go off on the next court and I wouldn't look over there. Well, maybe I'd glance. Or duck!

I'm dialed in. How that happened I don't know. My take is, it's what I expect of myself. And I think that's what I always come back to, what I expect of myself. If that's what you expect of yourself, you know that's going to flow to your students. You can't be singing one song and be showing up late, making excuses, messing around and not motivate.

From 1985 to 2003, I pretty much just worked with nationally-ranked juniors and touring professionals. Also, I would enter into contractual relationships with kids who I thought could be great, like a Jennifer or Venus or Serena. Not just good but great. Mostly Americans, some foreign players, but I was very open to diving in head first since most couldn't afford it. I just put in the sweat equity and just worked on future earnings once they turned pro. In 2003, I decided to stop doing this (which was bad for American tennis) and decided to help anybody anytime any age, even though the best of the best talent in this country needed developed, molded and identified. I decided to change the channel, and it was the best and most gratifying decision ever. Most of the I-will-pay-you-later deals never work out. Period. Since that time of making myself available to more than just nationally ranked kids or a potential superstar, it became even more gratifying and fulfilling and the parents appreciated it even more. The downside was many top-notch American prospects who maybe couldn't afford the academy or private lessons didn't have the opportunity many did in the '80s and the '90s. The ones that could afford it and wanted one-on-one privates continued and does to this day. But I didn't seek and scout talent and wasn't on a mission to find the next Serena or Andy.

I never really wanted to travel and go on tour. Coaching a top 10 player in the world I would have only done if I started with them at a young age. I have been asked many times but always said no. I would rather bake the cake instead of just put the icing on it. That is me. Now if I could bake it and then put the icing on, that is real and to me it tastes better. At the pro level, it is more of a manager/supervisor/friend than sometimes a coach. A lot of ex-players like that and they eventually go from player to player, it seems, especially after a few bad losses! Remember, you can't fire the player! The player has been built from the influences good or bad they got at a young age, so in the pros it's more the mental and strategic part that needs to be addressed. Not always but most. Plus there are so many people just hanging around the player, and the entourage is really sometimes silly. Plus many moms and dads become the coach. How crazy is that?! Only in tennis! It is easier now because the real dirty work has been done, especially in tennis more than any other sport. It is such a skill sport. The cards you're dealt good or bad at a young age, they are usually what you play with. But you're just bigger stronger and hopefully smarter!

In the pros, it is amazing the amount of technical flaws that are never getting corrected, especially on the serve. Things happen so fast the human eye just can't see it. Coaches can't, television commentators can't. Most don't understand the biomechanical concepts of what should happen. and most of the time the real big ticket item on the serve, especially on the women's tour, is the timing of the leg drive to create the racquet speed. When you talk about timing it is a slippery slope, but exact synchronization of when the racquet should enter the back area is way, way off, even if somebody hit 120 miles per hour! Well into 90 per cent of the players, even ones that win Grand Slams tournaments or we think they have a great serve, have left enormous racquet head speed off the table. Especially on the second serve where there is most tension/fear/choking and the players just enter way, way too early and the legs and racquet almost push up at the same time, which is the exact opposite of what should really happen. It should be counter intuitive as the legs should drive the racquet into that area. Some enter 20, 30, 40, 50 percent too far before the legs drive. You can still serve but just will never make it the best you could have. This is the No. 1 problem globally in all levels, even on the pro tour and more on the WTA. I feel the amazing Venus could have hit 140 on the first serve and her second could have been 100 to 105 on a regular basis if this was ever addressed. Never ever was. She had the body and the linkage to do it, but it was never pointed out. V is one of many whose serve works, but massive power and spin was left in the dugout! Or it wasn't even brought to the dugout! This can be corrected very easily and pointed out with 3D technology or a human eye that is looking for it and understands the core principles of how it works.

It's interesting because technical adjustments of the swing happen daily on the PGA Tour and it's usually backed up by science. On the ATP and WTA

Tours, very seldom are major technical adjustments made, and if so it is usually the wrong medicine. Not just the limited biomechanical knowledge of the travel coach but a lot of tour players just don't want to tweak or change technique.

A really big thing that's helped me more than anything is those principles that were instilled in me as a youngster through my experiences and appreciation for everything every day. I feel fortunate and feel lucky. I never look back. The rear view mirror is in the garbage can. I've got to get better tomorrow. I will do better tomorrow. I expect to get better tomorrow.

When you're sitting there and have won Coach of the Year eight times, you've done this and you've done that, in other people's eyes they look at you like you've done this and it's pretty much you and Nick Bollettieri. That's all nice that people would think those things but I'm just thinking about who I'm going to coach this afternoon because I've got to be the best that I can be because that's what they expect. And more importantly that's what I expect.

Also for whatever reason I don't wear a watch. I haven't worn a watch on court in 25 years. (Maybe I think it will affect my timing. Ha!) I can just tell the time by the sun. I'm just out there, I just know it. I've been on the court for so many years I just have a feel for the time. Plus the sun is a lot cheaper than a Rolex! Here is a great piece of advice that is very real: If you keep looking at your watch because you want something to end or be over, time goes slower! Please don't look at your watch. Time will go faster. Embrace what you're doing right now. Love it. Be passionate. Try it. Time tells all. By the way, time to go.

To do so much with so little, I feel good about that, where I came from, what I've done. But I'm not saving anybody's life or anything like that. I teach the game of tennis. When people want to introduce me, I say introduce me as one of the guys. I'm just one of the guys. The rest is foo foo. That's me. Perception might be different because of what I've accomplished and who I taught and all that stuff. I think because of that approach I spend a lot of time with people, I answer all the e-mails, I talk to people, I like doing stuff for others and people appreciate that because of that personal touch. At the end of the day they want you to influence your child with tennis, and when they come to me I always want it to be not only about the instruction but they're going to get a lot more than tennis no matter what level they're at that they've never gotten. But they're going to get so much more future stepping stones that are going to benefit them not only in the game of tennis but how this thing plays out the rest of their life. A good coach can change grips, strokes, movement. A great one can change lives.

2

IT IS IN THE EYE
OF THE BEHOLDER

Evaluating talent in my opinion is a real art. Everything in life is in the eye of the beholder, whether it is football, basketball, baseball, tennis, hockey or golf. People see what they want to see. People gain their knowledge whether it be from reading, watching television, their own life experiences and just what they've been used to. And that's kind of their baseline, or their reference point, on how they come up with assertions or assumptions, or how they see things. No one in life has a crystal ball, and obviously if it's a sport or a field you've done for a long time, your ball is going to be a little more crystallized than others.

It's interesting because I've heard many, many people say they have a lot of talent, they're fast, they're going to be big, they're strong, they have great strokes, whatever. People can't predict stardom or predict how good someone is going to be. There are so many mitigating factors when you're dealing with children that nobody knows what's inside someone's head. There are also too many speed bumps. Life throws you too many curve balls. It's a dress rehearsal each day. Life -- you don't know what you're going to get. So to say you can mail it in and say someone's going to be the next Roger Federer, the next LeBron James or the next Wayne Gretzky, it is almost impossible to do that. But some have an eye, a vision, a feeling, and a gift to see the future.

The main reason why athletes improve is, No. 1 they have to have an enormous burning desire to work hard. If that's not there, I don't care how talented you are, some day, somewhere, somebody, it will beat you. If you don't work hard at anything, nothing's going to happen. You can acquire that. It doesn't mean you have to have that at age 8 or 10 or 12. You can acquire that. It's a long-term process but it still helps to acquire those habits at a young age. If you're used to things being given to you, or you had the opportunity just because of finances, or someone had the knowledge to help you, that might be why you're good at a young age. You just had a better opportunity to get better sooner.

I like to tell people it's not where you start, it's where you finish. It's a long-term process. Athletes in general, when you're looking at someone, the first thing you always want to digest is the genetic background, whether it be the mom, the dad, the grandma, the aunt, the uncle. Genetics play a big role in this. It just blows me away that people don't understand that.

It's interesting that two of the best women that ever played tennis live in the same household -- Venus and Serena Williams. The best doubles team of all time, they're twins (Bob and Mike Bryan).

You see it all the time. A guy played in the NFL, now his son does. A guy played Major League Baseball, now his son does. Same in the NBA. You were great in track and field, and now your daughter is an Olympic swimmer. It's amazing when you look at world-class athletes, more than likely -- and I'm not saying it couldn't happen -- but the genetics play a major league role in your specific athleticism.

So that's the first thing that I look for. Period. This doesn't mean that's a given. You might have gotten a certain kind of genetics that aren't conducive to your sport. I've had people that their mom won the 800 meters and was seven-time world champion and her daughter has those long, slow, gliding muscles, but her ability to get in and out of the corner on the tennis court looked like she had a broken leg. Yet if I wanted her to run from here to California she'd still be running. She seemingly had two hearts, two lungs, and once she got going it was see you later! But she never got that fast twitch. Her brother, who was the No. 1 hockey player drafted in the NHL, got the fast twitch. And he could go from A to B quicker than you can say A to B.

Genetics play a big key in this thing. So in evaluating talent, that's huge. Just because you can make 20 jump shots in a row at age 12, or you can throw a 90-mile-per-hour fast ball at age 12, or you're No. 1 in the United States at age 12 in tennis, all it means is one thing: You're the best in your age group at that time. Or you're the best in that tournament. That's all that stuff means. Period.

Now it's better than not playing at all. It's a nice start, but you've got to look through the evaluation of the result. First, I look at the genetics. How do they move? How do they stop? How do they start? How big are they going to be? Maybe instead of growing up they're going to grow out. That could be deadly, besides not healthy. You really need to look deeper inside and kind of forecast the future on how the size and the weight is going to affect the movement part of it.

Besides the work ethic, which I said was just gigantic, there's the attitude. Some people want to continue to grow and learn, some people want to get smarter, some people think they know it all. Believe me, the smartest people keep wanting to get smarter. The best people just want to keep getting better. That's a mindset, that's an attitude. You don't know how that's going to play out when people get older. The mind always will control the body and choices, and beliefs influence our wiring, good or bad.

We can sit here and say, "I can't believe this one didn't make it" or "That first-round draft choice in the NFL, how come that guy made it and this guy didn't? He was 6-4, he was 240, he could throw it 80 yards, he broke all the records in college but he's a bust in the NFL."

Well, let me tell you something. Most sports, as you go from juniors and college to pro, the speed of the game gets faster. Every athlete will tell you that. How that affects your nervous system, and how you make decisions is huge. You've got to be able to have a mind that can slow things down, and maybe you can never just do that. That might make you scared, make you afraid, and that could make you then hit the ball late or hold onto the ball too long or affect your balance. Or make you afraid of getting hit. You just don't know how that's going to impact you. When you look at evaluating talent you can't be caught up in the moment. There are all these other factors that go into it that we just don't know.

You could be the No. 1 junior in the world in your sport, but you just don't know what's going to happen. Look at Michael Jordan. He got cut from his basketball team when he was a sophomore in high school. I'd hate to be that coach. Maybe indirectly he did M.J. a favor and that made him work harder and get rougher and rougher! At the end of the day Jordan is the best basketball player of all time. Period. No one knew what's inside of him. I'm sure he was pretty quick and could jump and had a decent jump shot, but at 15 years old getting cut from your team -- to me that's huge. It shows us all it is not where you start, it is where you finish. Never ever give up! Never!

You also can't pass 100 percent judgment on children. You just don't know where this thing is going to go. When you look at evaluating talent, a perfect example is Jennifer Capriati. There was no doubt in my mind because of the following factors:

1 - She played with a low center of gravity, so when the ball came back she could negate the power with the way she was always low to the ball.

2 - She had great mechanics. What I mean by that is, in the game of tennis great mechanics last a lifetime. But that's in the eye of the beholder too. What are great mechanics? Also bad mechanics last a lifetime. So I knew technically she had it. I knew she had the balance. I knew that she could compete. And back then the speed of the game wasn't like it is today. I knew that she would be bringing a different style, an authoritative style that could still match up. And I already knew at a young age how she loved to compete.

So when I could sit there and say when she was 12 years old "mail it in" -- she'd be one of the best in the world -- she had a lot of those bases covered. It was the same with the Williams sisters. I just knew because of how big they were going to be and how fast. The women's game had never seen it. If they could just get those strokes, they had those key elements. I knew they had that hunger because they wanted to succeed because they had nothing. They had that drive to want to do it. We were on a mission and they had athleticism that the sport hadn't seen yet. Size, speed and power. They were competitors first and tennis players second. That is the real key!

With a boy in any sport, not that it's a little easier for the girls, but there's not the physicality that you get with a girl that you do with a boy. In evaluating talent, there are so many factors that go into this. You've got to be real careful in evaluating a boy in any sport. The physical aspects and maturation come later down the road. That to me is a game changer. But how they compete, to me, is critical. Some people can have all the physical attributes and qualities but just the way they compete could make them just a good college player. It's such a long-term journey when you're evaluating talent, especially when they're young. You have to love pressure. Not like it, love it.

It's interesting in the game of tennis -- which I believe is one of the most difficult of every sport out there -- in the women's game you have a better chance to do adult-like things at a young age than probably any other sport except for maybe gymnastics and diving. With tennis, it's very easy for me when these kids are younger if they have a few key elements covered. To see greatness first and foremost, it's always the movement. And then since tennis is a skill sport it's the technical base. That's what is tricky because the way the game is played now is different than even 10 years ago. And great technique is essential so that it doesn't break down with the speed of the game. It is now a game of emergencies and you have to have the ability to improvise 24/7.

This is a true story I got from parents in trying to evaluate talent: They wanted me to coach their daughter. The mom was a world champion sprinter and father a world champion discus thrower. Obviously there was great athleticism and wiring more than likely in their daughter. It was such a great base to start from. They started right off with wanting to do a long-term contract and me taking the risk and coach her for free. I said, "I don't really do those deals any more as they almost always blow up or just don't work out. But I will take a look as the genetics could be very intriguing."

I set up a visit for them to attend the academy and then I asked about tournament results and exactly what is going on. They said, "Well, Rick, she is only six months old and she is hitting balloons above her crib, 100 in a row and more, and she follows through and hits the balloon with both the forehand and backhand! She is always smiling and has blonde hair and blue eyes and will be very marketable!"

I said, "OK, great, but isn't she too old? Ha!" I told them, "Here is my advice: Call me in four years and save the balloons for her first birthday, and for now I'll work on a diaper sponsor!" This is the crazy world I live in and I get stuff like this always. Always!

If I see someone with a bizarre backswing or crazy grip, they might be able to get away with it but they will not be great. A weakness always breaks down under pressure in any sport. So if you have a great foundation, your stroke will not break down under pressure. That's why it's critical in the game of tennis that the biomechanics are rock solid. If you can put the technical part on someone who is athletic, who loves to compete, and you can tell by the look in their eyes — and in the women's game because there isn't as much physicality, even though there's more physicality than there was 10 years ago — it's a little easier to evaluate the future than, say, pro football or basketball.

Also when you're talking about pro football or basketball, a lot of these guys were the best. They're not just the best on the high school team, they're the best on their college team and they get drafted and all of a sudden they go sit on the bench. Some people can't handle that. That's like a left hook. Some people get more determined, work harder. Others don't. They say, "Hey, I got my couple million." And people change. You don't know what's inside someone. It's always a roll of the dice, and it's not an exact science and you're just hedging your bet on these things.

And a lot of times, unfortunately, it's not even the player's fault. They don't get opportunities because of the system they're in, or the other players that are there, or injury sidetracks them, or something traumatic happens in their family. It can make people make a left turn. Some people may get around the wrong people and make the wrong choices and they go south, way south. And they had it all. Some people just kind of stay the same. They keep improving a little but maybe they didn't have some of these key elements that it really takes to be special. But most of the time, it is attitude. And an unreal positive one!

At the end of the day, in no matter what sport, it's a package. And the package is from your head to your feet to your hands. But what people don't understand is that they don't know what's inside someone. And what's neat about being an athlete. You can put whatever you want inside of you if you decide to make that choice. As a coach or a role model, if you can get someone to understand that, to keep trying to improve every day and look at it like that instead of thinking they were anointed or they're going to be great or they think it's going to be easy and they can mail it in, then in my opinion the attitude always determines the altitude.

If you have the physical capability, your attitude will determine everything. The best of the best don't make excuses. They always want to keep getting better. You can go through every sport and the best of the best are the most positive people and think differently! They keep training their mind as much as their body. It is about the wiring if you want to be the best you can be and extract greatness. Greatness looks over their shoulder so nobody sneaks up on them!

The greatest thing that ever happened to me in my career was in the early 1980s when I met a sports psychologist named Dr. James Loehr. He had such a profound effect on me. Words can't really describe it.

His research and his dedication to the field of sports psychology and mental toughness has pretty much become legendary, and it had such a dramatic effect not just on the game of tennis but athletes around the world. His influence on me has been major league. He had a systematic formula to try to get to the ideal performance state for what mental toughness is all about, kind of a step-by-step playbook or game plan of how to control your mind and not let it control you -- plus all the rituals.

It just dovetailed so much with how I was wired and how I grew up with the mental toughness really being my calling card. And then I met Jim and played a lot of tennis with him at Grenelefe Resort and did on-court presentations with him for a lot of corporate people, which was called "Mind and Performance." We'd do this for CEOs all over the country. To be able to be involved in that, and have that relationship with him, just had a major impact in the way I always thought. And now to have it backed up with the top sports psychologists in the past century, it was huge.

I became so intrigued that whenever I played against Jim, when we practiced at center court at Grenelefe, I would use his own mental magic when I played against him because I not only wanted to be a good student of what he was teaching others, I wanted to show him I could slow things down in my mind. Jim had a huge serve. But sorry, Jim, at first it was coming at me like a BB! After a few games it was like a beach ball! Sorry buddy.

Plus the body language and all these rituals we were trying to help with other people, and the playbook that he kind of put together. It was cutting edge and unique. It just went hand in hand with everything that I kind of thought and just figured out on my own — how to handle pressure.

So without a doubt he's first, second and third of people who have had just a dramatic effect on my career, not only on the court in how I've been able to influence others but off the court in just the way you look at things. Thanks, Jim, for extracting greatness from me without even trying to extract greatness from me. You gave me more tools in my toolbox to use and I have used them in every way!

3

FLIP IT!

Having the ability, especially in competition, to do what I call "flip it" is really the name of the game. What I mean by "flip it" is this: In life what we see we observe and then we react. And a lot of times what you see or how you should respond, the feeling that you have inside triggers a response.

If you're playing the game of tennis and some guy hits a serve 140 miles an hour, the first thing you've got to do is slow it down in your mind. The first thing you might do is you probably want the guy's autograph! You're probably going to be scared, afraid or tentative. But if you think it is fast, that's the worst thing you could do. Believe me, his serve just got faster by your outlook. When you start fearing it or you respect it too much, then it just got faster. It got quicker, then you got slower. You're not going to be as reactive or as spontaneous. So you've almost got to do a 360-degree psychological spin and you've got to flip these things in your mind. Look at it as a challenge and flip it.

The great Michael Jordan, the more you booed him the better he played. You were probably better off just sitting on your hands and not doing anything. He mastered flipping it in his mind. He loved to flip it! All great champions, and I mean the best of the best, Tiger Woods, Michael Jordan, they flip these things in their mind and look at pressure as their best friend. They love that stuff. They love the big moments. They love the controversy. They love it when it gets tough and they basically have no doubt and they flip it in their mind that they love it. They look at things as a challenge and flip it and the performance increases intensity and focus. They have mastered flipping.

People ask me all the time: How do you go out there and teach 10 hours and it's 100 degrees? The first thing I've got to do is I've got to make the sun my best friend. Believe me, after all these years we are amazing friends. I've got to love it when it's hot. It's the best thing ever. If I think it's real hot, it just got a lot hotter!! Smoking hot!

And that's the way you have to think of it as an athlete. If it's really, really windy and you think it's really windy, it just got really, really, really windy. So you've got to flip these things in your mind and say, "I love the wind. The wind's my best friend. I'm smarter than the wind. I have better footwork in the wind. I play great in the wind."

And if you don't take that approach, it is what it is. You're not going to change the situation around you, though you can change it on the inside of you.

But you've got to have the ability to flip it. And that's what a lot of people just don't get! They lose the mental battle before things even unfold. Or they're looking for those things as an excuse.

So having the ability to flip it and take a possible negative and turn it into a positive is a learned skill. It's an art. It's a training tool that if you could do it on a regular basis your mind would go stronger and you would become that type of individual. And that really centers on a big piece of mental toughness. And what flows with that also is having the ability to forget. To me, that is the most important asset that an athlete or person needs. And then you will look at the outside differently. You have to master flipping. If you can train yourself to have the ability to forget, you'll be the best you can be. I'm not saying the positive or things you have to remember, just the negative or the problems.

Everybody can remember the good things and stuff like that. It's how you use it that is huge. But having the ability to forget is also a skill. You watch any great basketball player, when they miss shots, the best keep on firing. They don't think about it. They have the ability to forget like it never happens. It's like a quarterback who gets intercepted and he starts thinking about it -- don't get intercepted or don't do this -- then he is probably going to get intercepted or be tentative or not let it happen! It's the same thing in tennis. You start getting a few double faults. If you start thinking about it, if you start thinking "Don't double fault," you can mail it in. You'll probably double fault. It is your fault for not flipping it! Ha!

It's a skill, period. The more you can practice that skill of having the ability to forget, every Monday, Tuesday, Wednesday, Thursday, Friday, Saturday, Sunday, the more you have that ability to forget and train yourself you'll eventually become that and think like that. You can extract more greatness from within by learning to flip it! Consistency daily is the key!

A lot of times people want to make excuses. And if you keep making excuses you get better at making excuses. So you keep all this garbage in your head on a regular basis. Not good. But having the ability to forget and not make excuses is a huge component because throughout the competition in any sport, you're going to fail. How you handle the failure is really the X factor. That really determines what's going to happen next. And that's the hardest thing to do, because everybody has a breaking point, everybody has a certain amount of thick skin. And at the end of the day we're all humans and we have emotions, we have feelings. There's going to be a profound effect on the nervous system.

If you can train yourself with the skill to forget, that's how you're really going to have your peak performance. That's how you're going to be in the ideal performance state on a regular basis, and that's how you're going to play to the best of your ability on a regular basis. But that is one of the hardest things to do, having the ability to forget because it's right there in front of you.

I like to take that even a step further with a lot of the players I coach. I like to tell them you've got to look at these things as a challenge. If you look at it and take a step back at it as a challenge and how you're going to respond from that, that's the first thing. Frame it up as a challenge. You've got to put it like a game within a game within a game. You've got to look at it as a challenge and then you're going to make decisions, because now it becomes a choice. And once it becomes a choice, you're looking at it black and white objectively. This is a skill and can be learned. It is a choice. Now it's your choice. Choice Grade A.

If you can follow greatness in other sports and see how they handle failure and see how they handle problems, there's a constant theme across the board. They're amazingly positive. They don't get too high, they don't get too low, pretty much on a regular basis. If they do get upset it makes them more determined. They don't even want to be around the negativity, so they're making a choice because you're going to have a feeling go through your body when something bad happens, say a double fault or something that makes you frustrated or mad. That could (notice I said could) make you have less confidence or have fear. You're going to have the feeling. Now you've got to start training yourself and this can start at a young age. And a lot of times if you have the utmost confidence and belief in yourself, that can help you have a little thicker skin. But it can start today. Practice flipping.

You can train for these things -- how you're going to respond, how you're going to think, especially if you know that these things really affect your movement and your thought process. These things destroy talent on a regular basis, and you see it all across the NFL and NBA and the game of tennis, golf, whatever. Can you do all this when the fans are in the stands, the money's on the table, the lights are bright? That separates great from good.

The bigger the stage -- and you see it in all walks of life -- these are skills that you can train for as a youngster. And I like to really explain those things to the kids. Also what I like them to do is never what I call "Look in the Rear View Mirror." What I mean by that is, you don't really want to look back. The past is the past. Today is today. The future is the future.

You have to have ability to move on. Some things you can't change. You can learn from the past but it's gone. You've got to let go of things. People don't let go. People love to dwell in the past. They like to think about the past. Now if it's positive things that can lead you to greater things, that's OK. But some people are still mad 20 years later. Not good! They won't let go of things. I see this all the time in competition. It really impacts your decisions, your next move, how you play the next point, what happens the next quarter or whatever sport you're in. That's why when the game's over, it's a new game.

A lot of times parents tell me, "Rick, when my kid serves good he plays good." I'm thinking, "No kidding. I want you to tell me your kid served terrible and he played great." I've never had a parent in 25 years tell me, "Whenever my kid serves bad he plays great." That's what I'm looking for. I want you to serve a bad percentage and have your worst day and win 6-1, 6-1. Then I know you're winning with things other than your best weapon, because everybody can be good when they're good. I want you to be good when you're playing badly. "Well, I played great on Saturday. I moved great. I played unreal. Sunday I played awful." I'm saying, "Wait a minute. Time out. What does Saturday have to do with Sunday?" You have to prove yourself every day, period. Every day!

Now if you want the rear view mirror to have something to do with it, to make you feel better about yourself, that's great. But it's a new day. Every match takes on a life of its own. Every game is a special event. You can let things motivate you, inspire the way you think, but nothing has anything to do with anything other than the moment. It has nothing because when you're dealing with human beings and emotions, that's what we call the upset. That's what we call "anything can happen." That's what we call "we shocked the world." And these things happen because we're dealing with human beings. It is the X factor! Flipping has a big-time effect on performance. Remember the best of the best failed so much, this is why they succeed!

If you beat some guy 10 times in a row that means nothing other than you beat him 10 times in a row. It has nothing to do with No. 11 unless you make it. Or unless you let it. You've got to prove yourself again. You've got to say, "If I don't play my best, I can lose." You've got to respect the person but not fear him. If you think "There's no way I can lose. I beat him 10 times in a row. This is going to be easy," trust me, a few double faults, a few mistakes, a bad call here and there and you lose the first set. Now all of a sudden you can't breathe and you're going to have a rough day at the office. Very rough!

And that's why mentally you've got to go out there and know it's a fight. Never look in the rear view mirror because the past has nothing to do with the future. Remember you've got to prove yourself each and every day. And if you can do that as a youngster and understand the mental part of competition, it's a game changer. It's huge. Your wiring as a competitor can be unique! You will extract greatness you never knew you had. Andy Roddick always had this. He was always about the competition. Period. I love Andy Roddick!

Parents tell me all the time, "My kid needs mental help." And then they're the first one that's going to spoil them or make excuses. And the whole family environment is kind of toxic because they mean well, they're trying well but they're creating a big, giant marshmallow in their family instead of a kid who's rough and tough and can handle things and figure things out on their own. By the way, marshmallows get roasted! Yummy!

So on one hand they want the coach to come up with magic dust and create some mentally strong player. Sure, if you have weapons, it's much easier to be mentally strong. But it has a lot to do with environment and how you're wired, because everybody comes in different shapes and sizes and different backgrounds and opportunities. I try to work mentally with the kids. Many times people have told me about the mental magic that I've done with their kids and how I have helped them better compete. I think that has always been my X factor, being able to motivate and explain things in a way that is a little different than maybe a guy who is a sports psychologist. I can relate and explain differently because I've seen it every way. I understand it. I know an enormous amount about sports and competition and can explain it and that resonates and connects with kids and players because they relate to the words I'm saying, where reading it or hearing it from someone else is always different. I think that has probably been my calling card as far as helping people psychologically in becoming more mentally strong and understanding how to flip it! And this makes them a better competitor, and that is the ultimate gift a coach can instill.

Years ago I was asked to do a big clinic at Westchester Country Club in Rye, New York, and I went up there before the U.S. Open and had about 35 kids on a court on a Sunday morning. Everybody is dressed in white and I'm there just by myself. There were no other pros. I said, "OK, I think this one is going to be a little bit more about demonstration and life skills and explaining things. I had all the kids on the court and was going through everything and was talking more about their mindset and how to compete and how to think, how to handle pressure. It wasn't so much about X's and O's and how to hit a forehand and a backhand or biomechanics. I talked for about an hour and a half, and probably about 20 parents were on the sideline, mostly dads. After it was over with, I find out almost every guy on the sideline was a Wall Street executive or CEO. One approached me and said, "Let me tell you something. I don't know if my kid learned a damn thing but that's something that's going to help me starting tomorrow. That was the best presentation I ever heard! It was crystal clear and so simple. By the way, I'd like to flip a few employees out the door!" I said, "Wrong flipping."

I saw another CEO on the golf driving range and he said, "Hey Rick. You have no idea how much you helped my golf swing. I'm hitting the ball so much better." I said, "OK, then the golf lesson was $300 an hour!" He laughed and said, "But I haven't putted yet! I laughed and said, "See, your attitude is already negative deep inside about putting. But I still like your potential."

That was pretty neat because I was talking about how to forget, and I was getting into all these triggers psychologically and here are these guys who are

CEO's of Fortune 500 companies just juiced up and they could really relate because they mastered flipping in the business world big time. One guy asked me to come and speak to 800 people. Talk about connecting the dots. A real winner knows what I'm talking about.

That was just from hearing what I was saying on a tennis court, how it really connects with business and getting people with their attitude in the right direction and how to handle situations. A lot of people get bogged down and start getting lopsided and go the wrong way. It happens in all facets of life.

So everything starts with attitude. That was one of the neatest things ever because when you get acknowledged from some of the best of the best in the corporate world that is worth a fortune. As in 500. Ha! And they're just hearing an hour and a half tennis lesson, and they come back with those accolades, I said to myself, I'm not only influencing a lot of young people's lives but even a lot of adults who have had a lot of success. If you can master or try to master flipping it, you can and will extract greatness from within that you never even knew was dormant in your DNA!

Here is a true story about when I was younger and competing: It was in 1979 in Willingsboro, New Jersey, and I was playing a men's open prize money tournament. I was ranked No. 1 in the state of New Jersey having lived there for a year before moving to Florida. I entered a high-level tournament that had a lot of better players from the Middle States. I forget what I was seeded, but it was a unique experience that I always look back on and laugh. I was playing in the final of the tournament that was held right downtown on the Fourth of July. Just when the match started there was a parade right by the courts. You could almost touch people through the fence as this parade was going on. There was the high school marching band playing the Willingsboro fight song. There were trumpets blaring, drums beating, people dancing and a couple thousand people flying through the street. After that there must have been five minutes of floats going by and a guy on a P.A. system screaming and yelling. You couldn't believe all of the insane noise. After then, there had to have been at least 500 guys on Harley-Davidson choppers going through the street and it sounded like 10,000 lumberjacks cutting down trees in a forest. It was the loudest stuff I've ever heard in my life. This was going on at least 45 minutes by now, fireworks going off all the time and it goes on and on and on. That was the backdrop. Right after the first game of the match the guy I was playing --- I forget his name but I'll call him Joe Psycho --- went to the umpire and said, "This is a joke. We shouldn't play. You've got to tell them to stop making all the noise. This is ridiculous. We should play in an hour once this nonsense stops. This is a joke."

Right then there was no doubt in my mind that I would win this match simply because of my experience of being able to flip it and my experience of just being around Jim Loehr so much early in my career, I loved the Willingsboro marching band. I loved the fireworks. I never had so many friends on Harley-Davidsons in my life. I love all these M-80s, silver salutes, cherry bombs, lady fingers going off. I loved it. I flipped it in my mind to the point where I embraced it. Because when it's all said and done, it is what it is. You have a choice. Macci loved it, Joe Psycho, well, went psycho!!

We were about even in ability but I won 6-1, 6-0. I blew the guy away in 45 minutes. As Mr. Psycho was getting interviewed after the match by the newspaper, he smashed racquets and threw his water jug over the fence and was complaining to the newspaper guys saying, "It was a joke. How can you play? This tournament sucks. I'm never coming back." The reporter then interviewed me and said, "You played amazing. That was unreal. Your opponent was so out of control, cussing, going crazy because of the insane parade and everything. How did you play so well?"

I said, "What parade?" ☺

4

ENJOY THE BATTLE

With so much expectations and everybody thinking that they're the next big thing in tennis, I've always tried to be very serious about work that has to be done and taking ownership. But also in the way that I try to connect with players and motivate and inspire them I always want it to be fun. I always want to create passion in them. I want them to have that enjoyment, the love to play and looking forward to coming to practice, looking forward to training hard.

I think that's a gift if a coach or teacher can instill that, then you've really created the positive energy factor in your practices. It can't be like boot camp where there's no having fun, because you're dealing with people. I think fun is the essence of getting the best out of your ability. When you enjoy something, you do it better. You do it because you want to. It is pretty simple. Few expect greatness from within. But fun and enjoyment create passion, energy and persistence.

A lot of people don't know how to incorporate enjoyment into the training, whether it be challenging them, rewarding or anything, whether it's prizes, food, T-shirts or even a five dollar bill. I think those type of things are very important, especially for kids to keep that motivation high. That's always been a staple of the way I teach, plus how I try to get the kids to just love to play every single point. Be all in. Every ball is the most important ball.

If you can get them to love to play and do it on their own, that's a big key if you want to extract greatness. Plus it's very serious because of the expectations and goals. That is the art of the deal if you want to extract greatness. If you can, then you've got it covered. You're going to get them to listen. You're going to get them to learn. They're going to do it because they want to and they're on a mission. The fire was to be lit.

You don't have to spell everything out. It's there. They'll figure it out. The key to being a great coach is knowing that. Just plant the seeds and let it cultivate and let them figure some of the things out. Plus it means more and sticks better when they figure it out.

Also you better make sure you pat them on the back. I think that it's more psychology, especially with the kids when they're younger because you want to keep them pushing themselves and you want to create that enjoyment so they'll eventually want to do it on their own.

Remember this is called junior development in any sport. It's not junior final destination. It's a journey and it's supposed to be development, like building a house. It should be serious. There should be accountability and ownership and all that stuff, but you're dealing with a kid and everybody needs to take a deep breath and remember, what was I thinking when I was 9? What was I thinking when I was 12? Always have that in there. But that doesn't mean you can't push and dig in there and try to extract more greatness. That's one of the things that kids want. They want to be pushed. They want to be told they can do more. When they do it, now you've got the big C, you've got the big confidence. When you've got confidence you believe you can conquer the whole world. Confidence extracts more greatness from within.

There's a game I started in 1985 that's pretty much legendary, if I may say so myself. I've done this across the country at every convention and it's really a staple of the academy. For 15 minutes in the morning and 15 minutes at the end of the day, maybe longer, you've got two people against two people and I feed the ball and I put people in positions where they've got to make decisions. What I mean is, they've got to let the ball bounce and they've got to improvise with their hands, with their creativity. They've got to handle the racquet like a magician but then the art of the deal is how I feed the ball, how fast I feed the ball and where I feed it.

The kids are learning how not only to play doubles but they're learning anticipation. They're learning about change of direction. They're learning how to pinch the center of the court. They're learning how to communicate. They're learning how to move because one of the most neglected things in junior development is pretty much the midcourt. I've always been a big proponent to have the kids do things that they're probably not going to do a lot of in matches or in practice. It's really neglected, like a lost art.

It has always been a blueprint of our training because the kids love it. They play it up to 11 points and you must win by two. When one team gets ahead to 10, I feed the other one a bunny, like a short overhead, and the kids have to play defense. You've got to try to steal some points.

It's very, very competitive and I'll put a five-dollar bill or a ten-dollar bill on the net strap and there will be seven or eight teams there and you'd think it was the finals of Wimbledon. It's ferocious and to this day I can walk into the players' lounge at the U.S. Open or the Sony Open in Miami and I hear people say, "Let's go! Let's go! Two on two. Let's go!" And every one of these players and many more who won national titles or became No. 1 in the world in the pros remember that game more than anything. How cool is that!

Not only has it helped people improve their tennis, singles and doubles, it's just amazing how it has helped their game overall. They had fun. They loved to hit the ball at the other person. They loved when you keep score and there's something on the table. There's a reward while the other kids are playing or jumping rope. There's this energy in the way I commentate, probably a combination of Dick Vitale and myself. I keep this thing revved up, very intense, really motivate, keep score and feed. Passion and energy breed more passion and energy.

It has been imitated but never duplicated! I don't do it as much now because I'm busy with private lessons, but when I do it's a special edition. I might do it at the holidays or when I have time. I've taught the other coaches how to do it. But after years of feeding and commentating, nothing tastes better than the original!

Developmentally, it's just amazing how people develop their hands, their feel and their head on the racquet like a paint brush. They learn the midcourt, the touch, the feel, the angles, the creativity. I remember doing it once at the Andy Roddick charity event in Boca Raton and you had Andy, Venus and Serena Williams, Chris Evert, Brenda Schultz and a few other top 10 players. You talk about a star-studded lineup! It was amazing! So I did this two-on-two game and it was so funny to see the Roddicks play the Williamses. They actually hit against each other when they were 10 and 11 years old. It was like Compton versus Texas. It was very competitive and you get an easy ball and you take the other person out. What happens is, you either get down low with a backhand grip and get ready or you're going to get a tattoo! A temporary one but still a tattoo! But good publicity for the Penn tennis ball!

Kids love it when you compete and there's a prize, whether it's a couple of dollars or a Coke or a T-shirt. You put something on the line and make it fun. It's amazing how that kid who was tired and hot or had a stomach ache and didn't feel good, all of a sudden they amazingly feel great. If you put something on the line kids have a tendency to find new motivation. I think that's a great lesson for any coach or parent. Make it fun and add unreal motivation and you can extract more greatness from inside. They have to enjoy the battle. When you enjoy the battle, you handle pressure better because you're all about the competition and just performing. This is when the mind and body work at a peak performance, when you're intense but calm. This is when you perform your best!

5

JENNIFER CAPRIATI

Jennifer lived in Lauderhill, Florida, used a Wilson racquet, wore Ellesse clothes just like Chris Evert, and kind of hit like her but with more juice. And I don't mean orange juice! She also played low to the ground and had unreal balance. That girl could play a match with a cup of water on her head and not spill a drop. She had just impeccable balance.

Jimmy Evert and her dad Stefano did a great job of establishing a rock-solid foundation. This was in the late 1980s and I thought all she needed to do was grow and not get hurt and some day she could be the best player in the world. She was a special kid. Even though she had a Chris Evert-type game, the thing that was a drawback was that her forehand was hit with sidespin, kind of like Chrissie's. I knew where the pro game was going and that it was getting quicker and faster, and she was going to have to have a forehand that had a nice tight topspin on it.

Jennifer Capriati

There was this girl Monica Seles training at IMG
Academy in Florida who was a pretty rough customer
coming up, and there was also Steffi Graf from
Germany. I just knew Jennifer needed to get a much
better serve. Especially back in the 1980s the serve in
women's tennis was just a means of getting the ball
in play. It wasn't a weapon. That was a Chrissie-type
of approach, because Chrissie had a great mind and
played amazing off the ground. But Chrissie was a
genius mentally with great focus and ice in her veins.

I made it clear to Stefano that you want this girl
to be Jennifer Capriati, not Chris Evert. She could
pick up on how Chris focuses and handles things but
after that she has to be her own person because the
game is much different. So through that relationship
with Ellesse they would come up every weekend to
Grenelefe Resort. I'd spend about 12 hours a weekend

initially with Jennifer. Her brother, Steven, would come up too. He was a pretty good little player, very quick, very creative. But he wanted to hang in the trees at this age instead of the baseline. We really developed a family-like relationship like she was my daughter. She was a great kid, very polite, always smiling and I knew she had the goods to be the best player in the world. No doubt! She was wired to perform!

She was also so appreciative of all we did. I cherish the Christmas card and hand-written thank you note she sent saying how she loved coming to Grenelefe and spending many hours of hard work together. Saying I'd helped her a lot, she said she tried to put 150 percent desire and effort into it and she would do really good the next year and be meaner and tougher.

Her dad wanted me to coach her full time, and after about a year they decided to leave Lauderhill and move to Grenelefe Resort. I got them a house to live in and provided all the private training and academy workouts and unreal match play. We provided the tennis component and she was put in a situation where we had so many good boys to hit with who were 15, 16, 17, 18. She had the best hitting partners you could ask for and she had the best coaching insight to develop her game. We had to tweak the forehand, get a serve that would be athletic, somewhat respectable instead of just getting it in. We also had to develop her hands, her feel, her touch because she was such a good solid ball striker. Her spin and grabbing the ball was foreign. I also had her play on grass a lot to stay even lower, move more forward. Jennifer loved to play on the grass courts with those laser ground strokes. She was Jen-erater!

There was one moment when I knew she was a tough customer and she had mentally what it took to be great. We were doing a drill one day with Tommy Ho and another top-ranked junior, and Tommy got a short forehand at the service line and Jennifer was at the net. Tommy uncorked about an 80-mile-per-hour forehand and it hit Jennifer right in the forehead point blank. It knocked her straight back on her butt. The racquet fell out of her hand. She grabbed the racquet, got back in the ready position, with a tear in her eye, and she said, "Alright, I know the rules of the game. Wait until I get a short ball." The look on her face was priceless. I loved that look as a coach and saw it many times in her career. Eye of the tiger to say the least!

I knew right then that she had the DNA of a street fighter and she was very competitive. When she got knocked down, her dad didn't come running on the court, which I thought was great. It showed me that she had it mentally. She always had a smile on her face, loved to play, and I knew that she really enjoyed the competition. I enjoy building and molding something that was already going to be amazing, but I knew this kid could be No. 1 in the world. There was no doubt about it. Jennifer was as close to a machine in every way possible. And a well-oiled machine.

So I only tried to take her game to where she played the ball very early, tried to be super aggressive. When she was 12 years old she started to win some 14s titles, and I told her dad, "Why don't we have her play the 16s in the Easter Bowl?" Stefano said, "No, I don't want her to get hurt." Denise, her mother, said, "No." So the moral of the story: I got her to play the 16s Easter Bowl as a 12-year-old and she was the youngest ever to win it. She didn't even drop a set. I think then people knew there was something coming down the pike who was going to be the next great American. I think people heard of Jennifer earlier, but when you do adult-like things as a kid, and you're that small and still a kid, the world should take notice. Winning the 16s Easter Bowl as a growing 12-year-old was the real first forehand shot across the bow that this American phenom was really special.

I told Stefano, "Listen, now you're going to fry the ultimate fish. I think we go for the 18s." And this was in April when she was 12 and they were against it. Everybody was against it, including the USTA. But it was more for her to test the waters. She had proven to herself to be one of the best 16 year olds. Just test the waters. No risk, no reward. I told her dad, "She'll get overpowered a little bit, but how close she plays to the baseline, how early she takes the ball, and even though she's 5-4 and 110 pounds she can negate the power just with the style of her play."

We enter her in the USTA National 18s Hard Courts in San Francisco where she's unseeded. What happens is, in four matches she wins in three sets but beats everybody.

She gets to the final and wins it becoming the youngest winner ever, younger than Tracy Austin, Andrea Jaeger and Chris Evert. She shocked the tennis world because this girl was smaller than everybody but she had it mentally and physically. Then Jennifer played the girls' 18-and-under USTA National Championship two weeks later. Bingo. Same thing. She wins the tournament and doesn't drop a set.

We get her a wild card entry into the US Open junior championships and she reaches the quarters and draws the No. 1 junior in the world and she loses a good, tight match. She could have won, but it was so hilarious because the stands were packed to see the 12-year-old phenom. What was amazing was that she was standing four feet inside the baseline to return serve and people in the stands were yelling at her, "Back up, you're in the wrong place!" Almost like they're coaching her because she was so little and young, she didn't know where to stand. Even agents were saying, "Why is she standing there?" I said, "Because she is supposed to, knucklehead!"

It was really the new breed, the new mentality because I knew she had these tenacious groundstrokes. She was one of the first with a lethal return of serve to take it on the rise and give them a nice surprise. And it probably opened some eyes!

As time went on, she started doing better and better and moved on to the pros. Just before her

14th birthday, in her first pro event, she became the youngest ever to reach a tour final (1990 Virginia Slims of Florida). The involvement of her dad was very unique. He knew he had a champion. He knew he had something special. He knew he also needed help. He was very supportive and a great guy. From my vantage point, looking from the inside out, he was also a great father. He always looked at her as a kid first, which I thought was very, very positive. He wanted to do what was best for her. And I knew any guy who would make a commitment to drive every weekend three and a half hours for top notch coaching, he was plugged in and committed. He was relentless in his determination and his daughter was that way on the court. A few times I went down to Lauderhill, but because I was so busy I couldn't go that often. But no matter, Stefano was always very supportive.

I think Stefano back in the day played some soccer, but he really didn't have that much of a tennis teaching background but learned a lot and knew a lot about competition. That was a big plus with me helping Jennifer because now we're always looking at the big picture. All I was concerned about was making Jennifer the best player I could because it's not about me or the parents. It's always about the player. They know what went into that situation not only mentally but technically. There were some serious tweaks that had to be done. That same summer Tommy Ho was the youngest to win the USTA National Juniors at Kalamazoo, Michigan, at 15, and Jennifer was the youngest ever to win the 18 Nationals at age 12. Twenty-some years later and those records still stand. That is scary stuff.

Both players, same coach. I remember as time went on I met with the International Management Group as they wanted to sign both players. We knew that Jennifer always would sign with IMG because they were going to play the Evert card. And I remember meeting with Bob Kain of IMG about eventually traveling with Jennifer, going with them on the tour and stuff like that and the same maybe with Tommy. Tommy was maybe going to turn pro also. We didn't know where he was going to sign.

So in the summer of Jennifer's 13th birthday in 1989, after she played the junior events at the French Open and Wimbledon, she returned to Florida back to the academy. Stefano made the decision to visit Saddlebrook Resort, where the USTA Player Development program was located. I even let him use my car to go over to Saddlebrook to look for a place to live. Now that's dedication. That's a friend.

I was a little stunned when they decided to relocate because Jennifer was like family and Stefano was one of my best friends. I remember that last day in the Grenelefe pro shop when there were a lot of hugs and tears and it was game, set, match.

But it was a great lesson to learn and here's what I learned: There was another bus coming because I know what I can do and know what I'm capable of. They really didn't have contracts with minors back then, so that was a little slippery slope because there was so much sweat equity, passion and determination put into the relationship. It was a little tough to digest. But it was a great chapter in my career and one of the most rewarding.

What was interesting is that the relationship that I had with Jennifer was amazing because I tried to get her to run through a brick wall and had a big influence mentally on how she fought and how she looked at competition, just her attitude in general. Besides there was the big adjustment on her serve and forehand, which became a totally different stroke, and just her understanding of the racquet. When she first came to me she was a little robotic but became more elastic and fluid. To this day her backhand was the most flawless piece of poetry in motion I've ever seen. You could mail it in!

People should really understand that her father Stefano was a great father. When it was all said and done, every decision was his decision. And as the parent, he made a choice to unplug and move on. Also with young girls, the father will always be involved, and I feel they should be. From age 10 to 13, unreal work was put in to help Jennifer -- specific, exact tweaking to help her really fine tune her game to be one of the best players in the world, to extract more greatness from within her.

After she left, a year later she skyrocketed into the top 10 in the world at age 14. I know what was put together from age 10 to 13 was a big key! Inside and out!

I worked with Jennifer again a little bit after she took some time off from pro tennis years later. She still had magic from head to toe and I believed in her. She still hit the ball as good as anybody in the world. I was one of the few probably besides her parents who saw her tennis future with a different set of eyes. And I knew if she really, really wanted to she could come back stronger than ever.

She was different because I knew how Jennifer Capriati was wired. Other than her mom and dad, I knew her better than anybody. I knew what was inside of her. You don't have magic in a bottle at 10, 11, 12, 13, 14 and make the most meteoric rise of any woman player at a young age, you don't have that gift from God inside of you and lose it. What you lose is a little confidence, a little fitness, a little self esteem. Jennifer really cared what other people thought. And that's a positive. I think any parent likes that in their child. Her wiring was a little different because she's such a good person and happy go lucky. She was an awesome kid!

When I worked with her a little bit when she was coming back, she was No. 180 in the world, and she would do things at No. 180 in the world that were better than people in the top five. But she didn't believe. When I'd tell her that's better than people top five in the world, that's better than Steffi, that's better than other top players, she said, "Do you really think so?"

I just knew as she matured more as a person and an athlete and got her belief back she would again kick butt. All the other media and tennis experts said, "No way." How did these people become experts anyway?

I felt she would come back because she had the game to play through anybody in the world and could go back into the top 10 and win. And she could win some Grand Slam events. Plus her dad was in her corner 24/7 and he could lead the way.

The game is only over when the athlete stops. I knew through Jennifer's inner qualities, her unreal drive, her work ethic, determination and persistence would be the driving force to become a major factor in women's pro tennis again if she wanted. And she did, winning the Australian Open and French Open in 2001, the Australian Open in 2002 and being ranked in the world's Top 10 for eight years.

People should never underestimate what's inside a champion. Jennifer's comeback in my opinion showed even more so how unique and gifted she was. It's a great lesson for anybody in any walk of life. It's only truly over when you quit, and there was not one ounce of quit in Jennifer Capriati. The kid is a flat out winner!

No one was happier and more glad than Rick Macci simply because I knew how special she was. With that talent, those strokes and that competitive fire, she deserved all the success she had when she came back. I thought it was the best thing ever when she won two Australian Open titles, the French Open, an Olympic gold medal and achieved the No. 1 ranking. And in 2012 she was inducted into the International Tennis Hall of Fame. People love comebacks and she gave one in the past century that was just unheard of.

6

ANDY RODDICK

John Roddick was Andy's older brother and I saw him play at the Easter Bowl when he was 14. He was a scary competitor. I mean he was Ray Lewis with a racquet. I got into a conversation with his parents and one thing led to another and John ended up becoming a full-time student at the academy. He attended his sophomore year and was one of the best players in the United States. What I really liked was his tenacity and the way he competed. In his senior year, his younger brother and the whole family decided to relocate from Texas to Florida, and Andy came to the academy when he was 10 years old. It was interesting because he was put into a situation where there were mostly older guys around John's age -- 15, 16, 17 -- but it was very unique because this Roddick kid was diminutive but very feisty and very competitive. I mean very competitive. I loved how this mosquito was wired.

I'll never forget one of the first things that he did. We always play flag football on Sunday. The ball was kicked off and we ran down there to get the guy and here's Andy and guys who are seeded players at the USTA National 18s and 16s Kalamazoo, some of best tennis players in the country and some who are playing on the pro tour already. And he goes down there and tackles the guy. He doesn't pull the flag, he tackles the guy. Gets him on the ground and then pulls his flag and he's got a pretty good bloody nose from doing this. He looks up at me and says, "I got the flag!"

I said, "Listen, we're not playing tackle. You've got to pull the flag out first, meatball! This isn't tackle." I knew then and there just like his brother he was just a tenacious competitor who had a lot of potential. But at the end of the day, it was more about his big brother who went on to become one of the best juniors in the United States and one of the best juniors in the world. Andy was in the academy and I became Andy's full-time coach. Their situation was very different than other players because the Roddicks were in a position where they could afford private lessons, and I worked with him pretty much every day. He was very much accountable for everything he did.

It was a little different than the Capriati situation or the Williams situation where they needed financial help. The Roddicks could afford it. From a business point of view, those relationships are much more healthy because if someone wants to leave or whatever, OK, there's no problem with that. It's business pretty much straight up and down.

Andy Roddick after winning the "Little Mo" Championships, run by the Maureen Connolly Brinker Tennis Foundation.

As time went on, I knew Andy was going to have a great forehand. He had a nice rhythm to it, he had a lively arm. I knew that if he ever grew, his serve could be gigantic. His mechanics and timing at 12 were so locked in. He'd be running around that backhand 24-7, even when he was No. 1 in the nation in the boys' 12s. You just knew that if he grew to the size of his brothers or bigger he was going to be a force to be reckoned with. He was wired to compete and had so much greatness inside he could extract.

We had a great relationship. What I always liked about Andy was that he was always competing. It was always about the fight. He loved pressure. He loved the battle and he wasn't caught up in the other stuff. It was really a tribute to his parents and the way the kids were raised because it was always about that. And as parents, that's what you want to instill into a child. It's all about the competition, doing your best and not getting caught up in all the silly stuff. So I worked with Andy pretty much every day for about three years and as time went on and he grew bigger, one thing led to another and he became the force that he became.

As I said, this situation was very different than the Capriati situation or with Venus and Serena just because it was just straight ahead. We want you to coach our kid. Work with him every day. And it wasn't so much about publicity or signing or for positioning, just make my son the best you can make him. I'll never forget when Florida State was playing Nebraska in football and the Roddicks were all Cornhusker fans. The game was in the Orange Bowl in Miami and I was sitting with all these Nebraska fans. The problem was, I wanted Florida State to win. Whenever Florida State did something good I got an elbow from the right from John and an elbow from the left from Andy. They were athletes. They were jocks. They were gamers, with sharp elbows! You get a little more of this obviously from the boy part of it, but in the end it didn't matter, they just loved to compete and truly hated to lose. My ribs are still sore 20 years later!

Andy became the world's No. 1-ranked junior and went on to be the best thing that happened to American tennis over a 10-year period. He finished in the top 10 nine consecutive years beginning in 2001, won the U.S. Open 2003, was a finalist in four other Grand Slams tournaments and was devoted to Davis Cup, playing for the U.S. nine consecutive years. He was all about the competition. He had very few bad losses. There might have been a few shortcomings in his game but he always showed up and he always competed. I think he had an amazing career and I think he maybe even overachieved. A lot of people disagree with me on that. He wasn't going to be Andre Agassi, he wasn't going to be Pete Sampras. He was going to be Andy Roddick and I think he really overachieved in a lot of areas. To me he is the best role model as a competitor you could have.

But because he was so good mentally I just have so much respect for him. I remember talking to him when he won the U.S. Open. He said, "I'm still the guy I was when I was 12. Nothing's changed. Everything around me has changed." Which is true when you think about it. It's about the court, the net and the ball and everybody's bigger and stronger. You've got more money but it's all about the competition. And I said to myself after hearing that, boy has that guy got his head screwed on straight. It's easy to go down a different path and start thinking all these different things. Andy was a competitor first and a tennis player second! Remember that.

Another thing I liked about Andy was it didn't matter if he was playing somebody 12, 15 or 18 -- he always thought he could win. He would always dive for balls, which I told him was not really recommended on hard courts. He was so feisty and like a little pit bull, or a really mean mosquito with an attitude that won't leave you alone. He just was there. I always felt that mentally he had what it took to be a world-class competitor. He showed consistency day in and day out, 24/7. He always practiced hard. He never took any plays off and he always competed. He never tanked, he never gave less than 100 percent. So he pretty much grew up with that being the norm. His thirst for competition, his drive to just want to crush people and knock people out was very evident at a young age. I loved how this kid competed!

I think that's really the X factor if you want to become a champion or you want to be the best that you can be. You look at his career, those staples, or that type of wiring that he showed as a youngster, that's really the X factor. It was interesting because as time went on after he left me, he kind of tweaked his serve, which really became cutting edge. He was one of the first guys to go out there that was great on the tour that had an abbreviated motion and their feet really close together. With me, he was in a classic position and had a regular take back but the same overall rhythm and biomechanics. He had a lively arm, even at age 10!

There's not a wrong way or a right way to do things as long as you're good at impact. And I think he kind of revolutionized a few things with the serve with that abbreviated backswing and modification in his stance. But everything other than that, the racquet speed and everything else that he had was identical to what we had him doing at 12. We put them in video side by side and didn't see any other than the stance and the take back. It was like a bigger, taller

Andy when you put his 150 miles-per-hour serve against his serve when he was a 12 year old. It was biomechanically identical!

His rise in pro tennis was interesting simply because with a boy you just never know. The game is so physical, it's much different than the females where there's less physicality. And you just never know where the boys are going to end up. A great college player? Maybe 200 in the world? But because he developed a weapon with the forehand and the serve and he had that competitive thirst. You put those three things together and that built the best American player in the last 10 years. And one of the best competitors in any sport. This was A-Rod!

Andy is not only a great role model on how to compete, but of all the players I have been fortunate to coach, his character, his respect, and his appreciation is world class. His roots have never changed. His parents instituted unreal values in him that still shine bright today.

In closing, when I told Andy to get the elbow up on the forehand at age 10, I didn't mean at the Florida State-Nebraska championship game! But, hey, at least he listened!!

7

VENUS AND
SERENA WILLIAMS

I was at the Easter Bowl in 1991 in Florida one afternoon and watching kids from the academy compete and someone mentioned to me that there was a girl out in California who had a lot of potential and had just been in the *New York Times*. I knew every kid in the country and I had never heard of this girl named Venus Williams. And they said, "Yeah, she's in the *New York Times* and there is a lot of potential."

One thing led to another and an agent from Advantage International said, "Mr. Williams is going to give you a call because they are eventually looking to move from California to Florida to come to a tennis academy." I said, "OK, give me a call." A couple weekends passed and Richard Williams ended up giving me a call, probably one of the most bizarre and interesting conversations I ever had in my life. We started talking and he explained to me where they're at, and so on and so forth, and he wanted to know if I wanted to come out to Compton and take a look at his girls. The only thing I knew about Compton was that it was kind of a rough neighborhood back in the day. He said, "The only thing I can guarantee you is I won't let you get shot!!"

I thought I've got to meet this guy! I said, "Hey, it's May, it's kind of slow. I'll come out for a weekend." I was very curious because if someone was that good, from what other people said, I know what good would be. I didn't have anything to do that weekend, so I booked a ticket and flew out to Compton and got into LAX, got a cab to the hotel in Compton. That night Richard and Oracene and Venus and Serena came over and it was interesting because Venus sat on one knee of her dad and Serena sat on his other knee and we had this two-hour conversation. Richard was asking me all kinds of questions. He actually was very insightful because he knew a lot of things that I was surprised about. He knew who I taught and what I've done and which kids have won national tournaments, how many times I've been coach of the year. He did some homework, so he kind of had the pulse on my career.

The night ended and he said, "I'll pick you up at 6:30 in the morning and we'll go to Compton Hills Country Club and that's where we're going to practice." He picked me up at 6:30 in the morning in an old Beetle bus, kind of wobbling side to side. I got in there in the passenger side and there was a spring sticking out of the seat and I was afraid I would harpoon myself and be permanently injured. So I watched how I sat, for sure. Venus and Serena were in the back of it and there must have been three months' worth of McDonalds and Burger King wrappers in there, and many Coke cans and bottles, tennis balls all over. I asked, "Do you guys sleep in here?" He said, "Sometimes if I have to. Depends on the wife!"

We pulled up to the park and I thought we were going to a country club. He said, "No, this is the Compton Hills Country Club. I named it that." I thought this guy was crazy. And I was right. Crazy like a fox! More on that later. It was a park that had two courts and it was about 7 o'clock on a Saturday morning and there were about 20 guys playing basketball and there were another 15 people at least passed out on the grass. There was broken glass and beer bottles everywhere. This was definitely different than the luxurious Grenelefe Golf & Tennis Resort, where I was director of tennis. So it was really a culture shock to see the situation.

When Richard and Venus and Serena got out of the car everybody acknowledged Richard. They called him King Richard. They acknowledged the girls. They stopped playing basketball and parted like the Red Sea and we walked through the basketball courts to get to the tennis courts. They were very respectful of the girls, probably because of the publicity. We go onto the tennis courts and they're kind of like the courts I grew up on. They were broken, chipped up and broken glass was all over the court. The courts didn't need resurfacing, they needed to be blown up.

I remember Richard had a shopping cart attached to the net post and it had about 20 feet of chain around it. He got the balls from the car and it took him about 20 minutes to get the chain off the basket that was attached around the post so nobody would steal it. He filled up the basket with balls, and they were all dead balls. But I brought a case of new balls because I thought maybe they might not have the best balls. After we got organized and had all the balls in there, Venus and Serena kind of jogged around the court.

One thing I noticed right off the bat: Venus ran kind of different. She was very long, very tall and had strides like a gazelle. I said, "Ah, that's interesting." I was thinking she should run track and not pursue tennis. This isn't very common for tennis, someone who is spindly. She was like a praying mantis. There was a lot of length there in her stride. Serena was very stocky and compact as a 9-year-old.

I started feeding them balls. One blueprint in seeing a lot of kids is that I see greatness technically at a young age. I coached Jennifer Capriati for three years and biomechanically Jennifer was not only one of the best ever in those areas of the game, she was one of best ball strikers ever. So now I'm seeing these girls from Compton and they had beads in their hair and they were swinging at the balls and their arms and legs and hair were flying everywhere. There were elbows going right and legs going back, there was improvising all over. So cosmetically I'm looking at this and I'm thinking, "This is a train wreck! This is all hype and I cannot believe I'm in Compton, California, ruining my weekend." I didn't think they were really that good. I had seen all the kids and had just come from the Easter Bowl and I'd had many kids win every national at that time.

I thought Venus and Serena looked like decent athletes but technically they were all over the map just because they were improvising. You could tell they just didn't have quality instruction. After about an hour we started doing competitive things where Venus would do something against Serena even though Venus was much better at the time. Richard said, "I prefer that they not play against each other." So I said, "OK" and had one of them come and play with me. So we started competing and right then and there their stock rose immediately. My whole perception -- and this is a good lesson for any parent or coach -- you don't judge a book by its cover. I looked cosmetically and I saw what I wanted to see. And I come from a vast background of information and I passed judgment that I thought they were limited. Now when they start competing I saw the preparation get a little quicker, I saw the footwork get a little faster, I saw consistency raise a little higher. I thought, "OK, they went from just maybe average kids their age to they could be some of the better prospects in the country." At least now their stock was at a point where I thought they're good, there's some potential here. Athletically they were unique for sure.

But technically they were still a train wreck. Just a lot of things were really way off. They hadn't had world-class instruction. But the way they competed, and they didn't want to lose the point, to me their stock rose even more. To me that's always the X factor, the way someone competes. Venus and Serena had a deep down burning desire to fight and compete at this age. It was unique. Unreal hunger.

Then Venus asked Richard if she could go to the bathroom. There was a lot of hugging and kissing going on. There were a great close knit, loving family. So Venus decided to go to the bathroom. She went out the gate and the first 10 feet she walked on her hands. And the next 10 feet she went into backward cartwheels.

Now I'm seeing this girl and I'm thinking, "How tall are these girls going to be?" He says, "They're both going to be over 6 feet, strong and powerful." And I said, "Let me tell you something. I think you have the next female Michael Jordan on your hands." And he put his arm around me and he said, "No brother man, I've got the next two." At 10 and 9 years old.

Venus comes back and we do more competitive drills. And as the day goes on I'm thinking, 6-1, 160, strong, powerful, fast, these girls can transcend the game, period. And it's not one, it's two. They both can be better than Capriati just because I can help them with advanced technique and footwork, and because of their athletic ability the sky is the limit. Maybe outer space, near Venus! Ha!

Athletically, I felt the game of tennis had never seen anything like this. Usually if you were big you were clumsy. If you were strong you were clumsy. They were going to bring something to the game of tennis that the world had never seen, someone who is big, strong, and fast. I knew there was something unique there. We could transcend the women's game. I was going to be all in.

But their serves were messed up as were their volleys and grips. That alone needed reconstructive surgery. That's something that with a lot of work you could do. You can't teach size, speed and how they fought at such a young age. In my eyes, they were just very unique.

We continued the full day and went out to dinner and really bonded. I really liked Venus and Serena. They were nice kids. I thought that Richard was very, very bizarre, to the point where the following day, Sunday, we practiced and before he took me to the airport he said, "I've got to interview you." I said, "Alright." So we put two chairs on the court, he pulled out a camera on a tripod, pulled out a piece of paper that had about 50 questions. He was interrogating me. I thought I was taking a polygraph or something. He knew more about me that I did. He knew girlfriends, everything. And I'm just sitting there thinking, "Wow. This guy is amazing. If he's going to trust someone to come into his inner circle or become a father figure to kids, he is going to do his homework." I respected Richard Williams a lot.

Then he stopped the video tape for a commercial. He said, "This is being brought to you by Super Socko, the official drink of Venus and Serena! This is also brought to you by Reebok, the official clothing line."

I thought, "This guy is too much." I asked him, "Why do you do that?" He said, "Well, maybe down the road they'll sponsor me. Not maybe, for sure." How crazy is that?! It was weird. It was very funny. He was a nice guy and a great father. His wife Oracene wasn't really around that much.

At the end of the day, they take me back to the airport and I fly back to Grenelefe. Shortly thereafter, I had to go to Japan with Tommy Ho for an exhibition so I was gone for a few weeks. I'm sitting in my hotel room in Japan and all of a sudden I see Venus and Serena on CNN on my TV! I thought it was kind of funny and then Richard ends up calling me and saying, "We're going to make a decision where we're going to go. It's really between you and Nick Bollettieri. Our girls really like you and want you to be their coach but we're going to visit both places and we'll make a decision. IMG is going to give us a lot!"

Time goes on and they come to visit in the middle of summer. It's hot and they get an idea of what the camp is like and what it is at the IMG Academy. September rolls around and Richard announces at the U.S. Open -- why at the U.S. Open I don't really know because no one really knows or cares about his kids –

that they decided to come with me. The main reason was that because I'd coached Jennifer Capriati two years earlier maybe he knew I'd have the passion and drive. I knew it was going to be a major undertaking because there was lot of technical help. There was going to be a lot of publicity now that they have the same coach that had Tommy Ho and Jennifer. I knew it would all have to be pro bono, the rest was all on the back end and it was a risky proposition because of injury or you never know. But I believed that I had the No. 1 and No. 2 players in the world, and we went into a contractual relationship for future earnings and their results. What I didn't know is what Richard really wanted or what they expected. We got into the negotiations and there was a lady named Sally Sullivan, who was a Seattle attorney, and the late Keven Davis, a Seattle attorney. They were now involved in this process.

Richard was ready to leave Compton but he needed a way to get to Florida. So we're still negotiating the deal and they're ready to come. The first thing he wanted was a motor home. I thought they said they wanted to live in a mobile home. So I'm looking around Haines City, Florida, for a mobile home and wondering, "Why do they want to live in a mobile home?" After a few days I found out it was a motor home and I'm thinking, "OK." The moral of that story is I end up buying them a $92,000 motor home. I had to put $38,000 down. They bought it out in California and they drove it out to Florida. No matter what it took I knew there was going to be millions to be made because I believed. I believed in the girls, period!

So to invest hundreds of thousands of dollars to me was not a risk because I believed in three things -- I believed in me, I believed in Venus and I believed in Serena. And that's all the belief I need for me to go for it. So they got the $92,000 motor home and a brand new Ford Aerostar van when they got to Florida. They had health insurance. They had a place to live, a four-bedroom house, $5,000 worth of furniture. Richard was put on the payroll the first year and he got paid $54,000. They had their own two personal hitting partners all day long, six hours a day and 20 hours a week of private lessons, just one-on-one on a regular basis. They had taekwondo lessons. They had ballet lessons. They had jazz lessons. They had a golf cart. They had a membership to the golf course at Grenelefe. And the whole family moved, even the dog! I even bought Mr. Dog a bone!

I also provided them with Disney World tickets and food. They could eat free food in the cafeteria and the seafood buffet every Friday night -- a little different from Compton!

It was a major undertaking of about $150,000 a year that was being put out on them being at the academy because Richard didn't have a job, even though we put him on the payroll. But it was all for the future and as we kept negotiating this contract, the deal from my end kept getting worse. I kept giving more and more and the percentages kept changing.

At the end of the day it was 10 percent of both girls' earnings until they were 21, there was $300,000, $400,000, $500,000 when they won a Grand Slam tournament.

If this happened -- and I knew it was going to -- we were talking about a multi-million dollar contract for the money I put out, for the time I was coming out, for the sweat equity. Or the repercussions for my business because a lot of people wouldn't come perhaps because I had to spend so much time with Venus and Serena. You'd think more people would come because you've got these two little celebrities. But they were legendary before their time and a lot of people didn't like that. Other parents and kids were very envious.

What I was saying on *60 Minutes, Good Morning America*, ESPN, ABC, NBC over and over was, "They're going to transcend the game. They're better than Jennifer Capriati. He not only has one he has two. It's going to be the two best athletes ever to play the game." And I was pretty much going on the record to print and TV saying this when they're 10 and 11 because I knew where it could go. I had no doubt. I was on a mission to make it happen, period! It was going to happen.

So nothing was going to get me off of that because I believed in the girls. It wasn't because I knew I would get millions out of this. I mean, there's a business side to everything, but I did it because I cared about the girls. I wanted to help the girls. I wanted to help the whole family. And Richard and I became best friends. I was like the girls' second father. He very seldom lets anybody into that inner circle and he trusted me. I think that's the biggest reason why he went with my academy and had a contract with me rather than with something bigger if they had gone to IMG. He knew there was a lot of dirty work to be done. He knew that I was on a mission, especially after Capriati left a couple years earlier. And he knew I'd do everything 24/7 to make this happen. He would get my best shot, that's for sure. And you know what? He did!!

Richard profusely thanked me in a hand-written letter that I've kept over the years. He thanked me for my talent donated to his girls and himself, for being such a "wonderful person" and very good friend of his. He said there have been times that it has been he and I against the whole world and I always believed in his girls and he was so appreciative. He wrote that he looked forward to seeing me every day and that if his girls ever make it really big, he would love to share some of the bonuses with me even if I did nothing else. He called me a good father figure and said I am 10 times the coach that I think I am and Nick Bollettieri "can't come close to you." He said he would always feel I'm the best coach for his girls and he believed in me and I would be their coach forever.

We were working and working, and they're getting filet mignon and the best of everything anybody has ever gotten, in my opinion, in the history of tennis. There even were boxing lessons. I had the state champion in Florida in his weight division, Sweet Pea Cowart, who lived in Winter Haven. He was boxing the girls every day in a sand pit. They'd have to keep their feet moving nonstop, and if they didn't move they'd get a nice little pop. And I had the No. 1 nationally ranked kick boxer work with them. So there was an enormous amount of athletic enhancement drills done with these girls. Even though they were already athletic, my goal was to always make them even more athletic. They did the hula hoop every day. They threw the baseball every day. They threw the football every day. That's one of the things Richard liked, that I wanted to make them even more athletic.

It was a major undertaking to say the least. And because they were there, there was a lot of resentment. People were jealous. It didn't matter to me because I believed and I knew they were going to be the best in the world. I had no doubt! Plus, I liked the girls as just great kids!

They had everything at their disposal to maximize their ability. And as this was going on, the media frenzy took on a life of its own. We're not talking U.S., we're talking global. You name it, it went around the hemispheres because they were involved with me and there was more credibility to the story. And there was more of a baseline for the media to judge because of the years I had with Capriati. And now Jennifer was setting the world on fire and was in the top 10 in the world.

Serena, Venus and Richard Williams

Everybody is looking for the next flavor of the month. Everybody is looking for the next big thing and the publicity went to the moon. Or should I say Venus? And that alone is worth monetary value. Forget what I gave financially, forget what I did physically, just that alone put more helium in that Williams balloon, put more zeroes on that first deal that was going to be coming down the road. It was a game changer.

One of the things that's really important to me is that even though one day you're on *60 Minutes* or *Good Morning America* and there's all this puff and smoke, there are all these bright lights around you, at the end of the day you're talking about kids. You're talking about children. You need to have it fun. And that's what I really respect about Richard Williams. He let the kids have fun. He let them grow up and be teenagers and be kids. When they weren't doing their six hours a day with the hitting partner and myself working on the technical skills and all the strategic stuff, at the end of the day they pretty much did fitness.

And I'll never forget from early on how Serena was such a ferocious competitor. One of the things we did was play tag. It's very good for the kids to work on their agility, change of direction, first step, creativity so they can kind of go in and out, up and out. The first day she played when she went to tag someone she played with a closed fist! Yes, a closed fist! I thought it was hilarious. Here you have this 10-year-old almost like a little thug out there. When she went to get the person she wanted to make sure she got the person. That's kind of how she was wired. I think you can see that look in her today.

Everybody's competitive, everybody loves to compete or they wouldn't be in tennis or they wouldn't be doing something against other people. But one thing that greatness shows us, champions are wired a little deeper. They're a little more competitive. They extract more greatness out of themselves. What I saw with Serena early on was that her competitiveness was off the charts. I saw that with her playing tag. That just stuck with me forever, because in the history of the academy or anybody that's ever played tag that I know of, she is the only one that played with a closed fist. I told her dad, "Listen, she's either going to be an amazing competitor some day or she's going to get into a lot of trouble." I guess it's good that it turned out to be on the tennis court, not juvenile court!

Once they played an exhibition at the Family Circle Cup on Hilton Head Island, South Carolina, against Billie Jean King and Rosie Casals. They were kind of the entree before one of the matches. It was interesting because they're out there playing in front of 3,000 people and playing against two of the best doubles players of all time. I think Rosie and Billie Jean could see their capability, and Venus and Serena were trying to hit the ball right at them. They'd take a second serve and hit it right at them. They went for the jugular even at a young age, even though their shots didn't all go in but still landed in South Carolina!

After it's over with, we're going back to the airport and Serena is sitting next to me and Venus is in the back of the van. Richard and Oracene were in the front, and I'm hearing Venus in the back having a conversation about the match. I thought, "Wait a minute, is she talking to me or Serena?" I turn around and she's having this conversation with one of her dolls. "How you think you played, Venus?" She's going back and forth with the conversation with the doll and she just got off the court with one of the greatest players of all time. That really puts things in perspective. She's a 12-year-old kid who, when the bell rang and it was time to play, she'd go for the jugular. But now she is a kid. And Venus was a great kid! And I mean a great kid!

Again that's one of the things I admire about Richard. He knew they were kids. You've just got to let them grow up and be kids. It's not a race to the finish line. If you have that balance you'll have a more well-rounded individual.

One of my main goals, especially for Venus because she was a little bit older and a little more mature at a young age, was to develop a grass court game at age 11 at Grenelefe. In fact, the British press did a story on her written by former Wimbledon and U.S. doubles champion and freelance writer Angela Buxton. I was working with Venus 10 hours a week on the grass courts. I thought for sure she could win multiple titles on the surface at Wimbledon, which ended up being true. But I did the training more developmentally, not just for playing on grass courts. Venus had pretty big backswings and she didn't bend well because she was so spindly and lanky. I just figured developmentally, if she went on that grass court 10 hours a week, the ball skids and the player having to get down to the ball is a premium. You'll learn to shorten up your strokes, especially on the forehand. If not you're going to have multiple miss-hits and you're going to be late a lot.

At first, it was really a nightmare for her to play on grass, but as time went on, I could see how this was evolving. There was more compaction in her strokes, everything was simplified, and more importantly, I wanted to create a mindset. I wanted her to know if she hit a good volley on grass it would be a great volley. If she hit a bad volley it would still be pretty good. I wanted to promote the chip. I wanted her to learn how to slice the ball. I wanted her to move forward. But more importantly when she hit a good shot I wanted her to know in her mind how easy it was for her to run from baseline to net because her straightaway speed, I felt, would be by far the fastest the game would ever see. She could get from baseline to net in a couple of steps. And the minute someone got off balance I wanted to build a game where she would seek and swarm and really cover the net. That was kind of my goal. I wanted to build her game around her God-given talent. You can't teach size and strength. She was so long she would be someone's nightmare to lob over and she had such good reach. So the grass court kind of pushes you forward, makes you go forward, makes you run low to the ball. So I did it more developmentally.

That first year in 1991, her game just went to a whole other level not only because she was playing six hours a day and getting the best instruction of anybody in the country, but it was really honed in specifically to fill every little hole, to smooth out every little speed bump and try to address things because her backswings were big and there were a lot of arms and legs and hair flying everywhere. And playing on a surface that's that fast, like playing on ice, really helped her fill holes that she needed filled. I also got her to love grass. Just seeing how this played out over time, it was very interesting to look back and see at her young age. I just knew that she'd own Wimbledon. And she ended up doing that.

That was a huge part of her development, hitting on that type of surface and having that type of exposure physically and mentally to grass. Instead of someone saying shorten your backswing or prepare early or get down to the level of the ball, it was kind of on-the-job training. I think the best gift a coach can do is not sit there and show them how smart you are and how much you know but let them figure it out on their own. And if they don't, then it wasn't meant to be. But the good ones or the great ones always do, and that was a huge part of her development as a youngster. People have no idea how much time I spent with Venus and Serena. They just have no idea.

In 1992, we moved from the Grenelefe Resort to Delray Beach, Florida, and that's when the mechanics of the deal changed a little bit. Richard was getting $125,000 a year from Reebok. That was just for the kids to wear their clothes. He had to do a couple of clinics a year. Pretty much everything else stayed intact with the deal. As time went on and they got better, more of a cast of characters started to arrive. There were more stockbrokers, lawyers and other people getting involved. I could feel my place in the line starting to shift a little bit. Not with the girls but with Richard, because with Richard if he said "right" you knew it was left, but if he said "left" you knew it was right. He was pretty cagey about everything. He'd have a bad day or a couple of bad days, he'd get in the car with the girls and go somewhere else to practice. So he was always working it.

In 1994, the WTA made an age eligibility rule change where you could not turn pro at age 14. They called it the "Capriati Rule." They didn't want kids to get burned out and all this nonsense. I told Richard, "Listen, now you have to make a decision, your first real decision in this whole situation. Either Venus has to turn pro or you're going to let the WTA dictate to you how many tournaments she can play at 15, 16, 17 years old. Richard didn't like to be told what to do by anybody. He said, "OK, we've got to work on getting a wild card. Let's play."

And if they hadn't made that rule change Venus wouldn't have turned pro at 14 and made her debut. The only reason she did that was to get under the clock so she would be grandfathered in this rule change. So it was very ironic. That wouldn't have happened. She wouldn't have made her debut in 1994. History would play out a little differently. Timing in life is everything and determines everything.

Now the debut was going to happen. This was June and we got her a wild card into the Bank of the West Classic played in November of 1994 in Oakland, California, and run by IMG. I told Richard, "Now we've got to amp it up. We've got to practice a little more, turn up the volume, a little more intense." He said, "I agree. I agree."

The next day after this decision, Venus doesn't show up for practice. A day later he calls me and says,

"We're at Disney World." The guy went to Disney World for a week. I want to turn the volume up, he turns it down. This is Richard!

Then they come back and we start practicing a little harder, a little more focus. Think of it -- she hadn't played a real tournament in three-and-a-half years. She's playing boys and is getting bageled and getting crushed every day. She hasn't beaten anybody in three-and-a-half years. She has not won a match in three-and-a-half years in practice. She's played boys 16, 17 and 18 years old.

I knew when she made her debut that people would be very, very impressed in how she tried to play. But I didn't know if she was going to spray every ball out or if she would be so nervous she couldn't play. I didn't know how she would respond to the fans in the stands. But I knew all the players and media would see this girl for her coming out party and say, "Wow, I've never seen anything like that. Wow, she's tall and she has a great serve." And she had a lot of open stance, she played very different, but does that mean she's going to win? I had no idea. But was she going to be great? I said, "Yes, no doubt!"

We take her to Oakland. The year before, I believe there were 24 media credentials given out for the tournament, and this year there were 252. Venus was coming. It was almost like Elvis arriving in the building. There had never been anything like it. We go to the practice court on the outside and there are 300 people watching her practice. And she's out there practicing better than she ever had in three years. Venus was so ready to tee it up! I was so proud of her. She was stoked and dialed in! Venus Williams was ready to compete!

This was like a lion being in a cage, and now you're going to let this lion out and she gets to perform. I couldn't believe how she was hitting the ball with the hitting partner. She was so pumped up and I was really pleased she turned up the volume. The next day we were going to play a practice set and she'd never beaten the hitting partner named Gerard. I actually told Gerard, "Make it close, let her win in the tiebreak." Usually, he beats her like a drum 6-0, 6-1. They played and Venus won 7-6 and she had a smile on her face ear to ear. She was always smiling but she was so happy and said, "Rick, I'm playing so unbelievable. For the first time ever I beat Gerard."

So mentally she didn't realize that he didn't go 100 percent and you couldn't tell it. I don't know if Richard or Oracene could tell it but mentally I was getting her ready. I wanted that confidence to be at an all-time high. Venus was ready to go into orbit!

The draw put her against Shaun Stafford, who was a former NCAA singles champion who had been ranked as high as the 20s but was now ranked No. 57 in the world. She had a good serve, good power, but was a little inconsistent and had a shoulder injury.

It was a match that Venus was definitely going to get games. What was unfortunate, I just felt, everybody at this tournament wanted her to lose.

There was so much hype that this was the best thing since sliced bread and Richard could rub people the wrong way. And people love to see people fail in our society. Too much hate! Not cool.

She went out to play the match and Richard had her racquet painted with no logo. It was almost like "I'm available for rent." He bought clothes for her from JC Penney that had no logos. He might have put a "for rent" tag on there too! It was the funniest thing. All I cared about was Venus enjoying the competition and show the world her wiring and greatness.

It was an incredible thing. I can picture point by point even today this girl going out there running like Bambi and using an open stance on every shot and having no fear....just no fear. All in 100 percent!

Moreover, the match was played on Halloween night and the scariest thing out there was her serve. It was 115 miles per hour at age 14. (At age 10 it was 74.) She played so smart, so aggressive, winning 6-3, 6-4. When she won, she was jumping up and down at the net and there was a smile ear to ear. I had never seen her that happy! And everybody was in shock that this girl can walk off the street after not playing a competitive tournament -- junior, college, no matter, nothing -- right into the pros and beat the No. 57 in the world. It had never been done. It will never be done again. Now the media was going out of control because they're already anointing her that she's going to be greatest -- except the players. Martina Navratilova said, "Ah, she's tall. She's got a good serve. Wait until she feels the pressure." I'm thinking sour grapes. But I'm also thinking Venus loves pressure. It's her best friend. Venus is all about the battle. Bring it on. Pressure is Compton. This is fun! Pressure is an honor to a competitor.

Venus did the press conference, and it was all about her being happy and being 14 and loving to play and she really enjoyed it. But next on the menu was Arantxa Sanchez-Vicario, who was No. 1 in the world. Steffi Graf had a knee injury so Arantxa had moved up to the top ranking. What was interesting was when Venus played the match against Stafford she stood up the whole match on the changeovers and was bouncing like a boxer in the corner of a ring, because at the academy we never allowed the kids to sit down during practice. And there's a chair there on the side, as there is at every tournament, and Venus didn't even know what it was for because she hadn't played any matches! She just stood up and kept bouncing. Is that crazy or what? Crazyeee!

I'll never forget Bud Collins on ESPN said, "Her coach Rick Macci said, 'There's a chair there, you're supposed to sit down. This isn't like at the academy.' And now she knows what that chair's for." As Bud said, "This is unprecedented. It really sets junior tennis back. They might as well shut it down because no one's ever done it like this." He said it best. No junior competition in three and a half years. Stone cold raw and bang, bang, I beat No. 57 in the world!

The next day she plays Sanchez-Vicario and everybody is expecting 6-0, 6-0. I knew if she played her forehand 24/7 and just came in a little bit, anything can happen if someone feels pressure. Venus was up 6-3, 3-1 and I'm sitting there with Bud Collins and he said, "Rick, I'm telling you right now, this will be the greatest upset in the history of sports. Forget tennis. Forget Ali-Frazier. Forget the 1969 Mets. The history of sports. A girl walks off the street, never playing a junior tournament in the last three and a half years, never played a pro tournament and beats the No. 1 player in the universe. If you think of it in that context, it's make believe." And he was right. Only in women's tennis, because there's the age thing the kind of comes into play in that.

The next game was real close -- ad, ad, ad, ad – and she lost it. Next game -- ad, ad, ad, ad -- lost it. At 3-all, Sanchez makes a bathroom break and takes 10 minutes. Venus thought she probably left to go eat dinner! She didn't know what was going on. Venus is waiting out there, Sanchez comes back. I have no idea what happened. It was 6-3, 6-0 in about 20 minutes. Venus became a 14-year-old. But at the end of the day, she came to the net 33 times. I had her playing a game that was so different and people were just shocked. That night, both Nike and Reebok came calling. Seven or eight months later after a lot of negotiations and discussions Reebok won the sweepstakes and Venus got $12 million, $2.5 million a year for five years guaranteed. On top of that, she only had to play three tournaments a year. Unreal. Can you say lottery?

People have no idea after you've put four years into something and you do it, and this is the payoff. You see the joy and the fact that you've given your life and helped put together this unique athlete that you feel is going to be No. 1 in the world and she had the little sister coming up who could be even better. And to get this type of acknowledgment from one of the major companies. It was the largest deal ever for someone that young. And that's when the rubber hit the road, when Richard and I had to sit down.

Basically what happened was, he wanted me to give up all my rights to the contract from the past, which was in the millions, to have the opportunity to coach the girls for the next five years and he'd pay me a million dollars, like $250,000 a year. And then he said, "You're going to become famous." I said, "I don't want to become famous. I just want all the time and effort that was put in the past four years."

He said, "You're going to get endorsements because you coach my kids." Right then I knew it was over because when you go a lot on unreal trust and friendship and you're best friends and you're like a father figure, for him to ask me to give up the rights of what I'd put out and for what I did just to coach Venus for another five years, it was a left hook from Ali, to say the least. But it was tempting to want to do it. Yet the ethical part of it hit like a brick. I told him I couldn't. Richard got Venus and said, "You want Rick to be your coach?"

"Yes, yes."

"To travel?"

"Yes."

He said to me, "Are you sure you don't want to do this?" I said, "No, I'm not going to give up the rights to the past. If you're changing the rules in the middle of the game, I don't want to coach the girls under that scenario." As we know in life, money changes people.

That was really the only time I didn't agree with Richard. I'd always pretty much been there like his family and two days later I got something from him that I'm terminated and there's a settlement agreement, pennies on the dollar. And it dug even deeper. Then Richard buys a house in West Palm Beach, puts in tennis courts and hires a few guys from the academy to hit and now he is the coach. Ouch!

So for two years we went back and forth. Whenever Venus struggled they would call me from a tournament and I'd drive up to Palm Beach and meet them at McDonalds off the Turnpike and try to work a deal out. The girls struggled and Serena wasn't ready to play yet, and we could never reach an agreement because he just wouldn't come around after he won the lottery. He wanted all the credit and he wanted all the money. It was a little disappointing.

So I had to prepare a $14 million lawsuit, 164 pages, but it was never filed because after a little bit of time I couldn't get into a litigious situation because whoever has the most money usually wins. I wanted to be known as the guy who coached the Williams sisters, not the guy who sued, so I ended up settling for a lot less. How stupid was I! My wiring short circuited with that decision!

At the end of the day, I did what I felt was right. I only settled for one reason, because if I settled, Richard agreed, "Yeah, you're going to coach the girls again." And this was in 1997. I should have gotten that in writing before I settled, but once I settled then it really kind of went in the other direction. And he not only told the story to media pretty much that they went from Compton to center court, but unfortunately Venus and Serena were young and they didn't know a lot of details about the monetary part. It's a close knit family and a lot of times when those things happen they tell the story however they want. It sounded better that he did it all. He did a lot. So did Oracene. But so did Rick Macci.

I'm sure a lot of people in tennis know what I did, but they don't really know what I did. Forget the monetary part, the effort, 24/7, six days a week, just working those hours, trying to not only sew this thing together technically but deal with Richard because he'd be telling them a lot of things that were pretty much in left field. People said just dealing with him I should have gotten Coach of the Year! Four years, that's a pretty good achievement!

The moral of the story: after Rick Macci, no one really coached them. They made cameos at IMG

Academy, but it's like this in tennis: Some parents not only want the money they want the credit. Even Oracene got in to being the coach. I think from a support system, a belief system, eventually that's where the parent helped out enormously once they got on the tour.

Unfortunately, there are still holes in their games technically that they never really got sewn up or they could have been even better. Yes, better. I think Venus could have served 140 miles per hour if the serve would have been addressed correctly. I think they could have come to the net a lot more and played like I wanted to have them play -- seek and swarm. I think they could have had 20 Grand Slam tournament titles apiece. Don't get me wrong. They've had amazing careers. Through the end of 2013, Venus has won 44 singles titles, including seven Grand Slam tournaments in singles; Serena has won 57 singles tournaments, including 17 Grand Slam singles titles and both have been ranked No. 1. What they've done is great, but it could have been even better with that God-given talent.

Richard is a great guy and a great father. He just made a decision that was shocking to say the least -- that he kind of wanted to do it all. He had lots of ego. That's the way things go. You learn from it. It's in the rear view mirror. All I care about is who I have the next day and who I am going to teach. It is my wiring. It was a great chapter. I had to dig deeper to extract more greatness.

And you know when you did the best you could do, you know exactly what you did and the Williamses know exactly what you did, even though it's never been written about or told about in as much detail as I'm telling about it now. As long as you know you did your best that's all you can ask for in life. I gave Venus and Serena and the Williams family 110 percent and helped them when they needed it the most.

8

MARIA SHARAPOVA

The situation with Maria Sharapova was very interesting because of the success of Venus and Serena and how well they played right when they came on the tour. Venus with that open stance backhand set the world on fire by just playing a more athletic game and bringing a different style of play to women's tennis.

Yuri Sharapova, Maria's father, contacted me when he was at the IMG Academy and wanted me to take a look at his daughter, who, at the time, was 11 years old. I said, "Yeah, come on down and I'll take a look."

They came down and within 10 minutes I had no doubt whatsoever she was going to be a world-class player, even at 11, simply because of a few things that I could see. First off, her mom was pretty tall and her focus was amazing already! So I thought that would be a benefit to her serve. Her two-handed backhand was already timed and synchronized at 11. Technically, it looked like poetry in motion. I was really impressed with that. But believe it or not, her footwork around the ball, her little steps around the ball, was uncanny. The way she tried to get into position was really unique. I don't see that part of it at a young age. But in general her movement was average.

Overall, I saw some good stuff, but what was out of control was her forehand. It was very flat, to say the least. It was probably one of the weaker forehands I've seen ever on a good player or potentially good player ever. Her swing was quite big and the elbow kept coming into the body. The racquet almost opened up, the point of contact would shift on a regular basis. It was very, very problematic. I'm talking every fifth or sixth ball, she'd make an error or the ball would fly out. She couldn't grab the ball. Just the whole mechanics of the swing was incorrect. It was an issue, a major issue.

Her dad, whom I have a lot of respect for, felt he wasn't getting the attention at IMG Academy to the point where he'd get a hitting partner and go across the street to the high school courts. When Maria was 9 or 10, even though there was a lot of potential, she wasn't the flavor of the month. Even though people knew she had potential and she had good looks and there could be some marketing opportunities there, he wanted more. He wanted filet mignon. He wanted in-depth technical help, and he wanted someone to really coach his daughter. He just felt she was just hitting balls.

After the first couple of times they visited -- they'd come for a week at a time -- we discussed in every possible detail the possibility of switching her to play left-handed. Yes, left-handed! Yuri really wanted her to switch and be a lefty player. He thought it wasn't too late because she was 11. I have the video tape to prove it. We came to the conclusion that she was going to play left-handed. I said, "Yuri, this is a big jump. I know it could be unique, I know her serve might be a little more of an advantage," so on and so forth. And the reason why he wanted her to play left-handed and switch was because when she swung the racquet with her left hand it was once again poetry in motion. She hit the ball better, obviously not as hard. Her contact point always was in front and there were no hitches. She was very smooth, very compact when she hit lefty forehands.

He said, "Rick, I don't care. Let's go for it. I only care how good she is at 18, junior tennis doesn't mean anything. She has to get a forehand or it's going to be a roadblock." He was looking at the right picture because she already had good footwork around the ball and was going to be a great competitor. She was wired to compete and focus. I could see that already she had a great determined attitude to achieve. She wasn't fast and she wasn't too agile, but she was going to be able to hit the ball hard and pretty flat, so she could probably hide her lack of overall agility. He just knew technically if she could get better on the forehand things could be world class.

Maria Sharapova with her father Yuri

So here we are practicing, he's sending me tape when he goes back to the IMG Academy. I'm looking at tape, analyzing it of her hitting lefty forehands. Yuri is out there coaching her in Russian with the hitting partner. It's getting better and better. They come down for the next visit for a week, a month, and this went on for almost a year and she's getting a lot better. Then I tell him, "Listen, I don't think she should play left-handed because when I feed balls to her backhand, which is now a left-handed backhand, her backhand now looked very uncomfortable. Her backhand looked problematic. She was scrunched and cramped up when she hit the ball. Her point of contact wasn't natural. So it's almost like we've got the same scenario but on the other side of the body!

But it was a little more forgiving because she had two hands and she could improvise. I told him that was more of a strength thing. So we went back and forth on this issue. He really wanted her to play left-handed to the point where he called her agent. And he thought we were 100 percent crazy, and at the time they didn't want this to happen. And I really didn't want to make it happen but Yuri was all in on making it happen. I said, "We just do the best technical tweaks on this stroke. It's never going to be probably amazing but we can fill the holes and make it somewhat of a solid stroke. I don't think it's ever going to be something special but I think I can get it out of the liability phase." She just hit so many balls the wrong way. It was just bad flat out muscle memory.

When IMG knew that she might switch left-handed and that on a regular basis she was coming down to Rick Macci Academy, Yuri told them that they wanted to leave IMG Academy and do a deal with us. IMG didn't want him to move to the RMTA academy, but still Yuri wanted to work a deal out with me where it was all based on free coaching, free hitting partner, free fitness, and the upside would have been percentages and bonuses to the point of about $1 million if she made it big. I knew she could be a great player and I saw the endorsement possibilities because she was a cute little kid. You could see she had Madison Avenue written all over her. You get anywhere near the top 10 it's a good investment and a no brainer! Plus Maria was a great, super sweet kid. Her forehand scared me a little because I didn't want it breaking down every fourth shot. I saw Arantxa Samchez-Vicario get to No. 1 in the world with a very,

very bad forehand. So I thought Maria with her size and strength probably could hide it easier. When IMG got wind that she might play left-handed and that she might leave IMG, within 24 hours they flew down to the RMTA. Yuri said that was more attention than she got in the last two years. Even though they were still going to represent her, it was a little disturbing because at the end of the day they probably didn't want what was really best for Maria but was best for them. Maybe because of publicity they wanted the whole pie because they own their own academy. But Yuri wanted a slice of it with Rick Macci and RMTA.

Yuri wanted to leave. Maria wanted to leave because they had personal world-class coaching and attention to detail, and it was more of a family environment. One thing led to another, the weekend passed and everything seemed great. Yuri said, "We're going to go back and we're going to pack everything and we'll be back the following week, and we're moving her permanently and we're going to do the deal. We'll work all the details out with the people at IMG."

After they left the condo they were staying at, the housekeeper found a letter from Maria that she wrote to God saying she couldn't wait to move. She wrote that she loved it here and wanted to leave where she was and it was exciting. It was really interesting that an 11-year-old girl would write a letter like that. There was a bond that was created from start to finish and obviously a mega deal to be done. It might be five, six, seven years down the road. Other than what I saw in the Williams sisters, I knew there was a lot there tennis-wise and marketing-wise because she had the looks and would have the game! Most of all the wiring and focus was special. I could help extract even more greatness.

A week passed and I kind of felt uneasy because I knew once they went back to the other side of the fence there was going to be a full-court press in for them not to leave. The moral of the story: Yuri calls me up and says, "We can't leave. IMG doesn't want me to leave. If I leave I might not get wild cards in the future, I don't want to get blackballed. They're giving me more money to stay. They guaranteed I'd get better matches. They're guaranteeing I'm getting better hitting partners." It was the whole song and dance.

I just said, "No problem. Anything you need."

He said, "They don't want me to come here."

I said, "Listen, I love your daughter. She's a great, great kid. You and your wife just understand it's a journey and a long-term process and you have the thoroughbred to make it. Here's what I recommend… you've got to get technical help. If they're not going to let you come here because I have an academy and they don't want, for whatever reason, the publicity, even though the coaching she needs right now is technical, I would make them pay for her to have technical help on the forehand. And if you want I'll give you the phone number."

Which I did. I said, "There's a guy in California named Robert Landsdorp, I would call him. He can teach your daughter how to hit the ball cleaner and he can probably connect the dots better than probably anybody in the country. He's not going to make it perfect because I think there's too much damage done. But 24/7, she needs a forehand."

The moral of the story: She goes back, she stays there, whips out to California now and then, IMG picks up the tab because Robert doesn't have an academy and she just gets technical help. IMG Academy still gets the credit. They still represent her and that's how that whole thing played out. That's a story that's never really been told because I have so many stories like this, not of people who went on to become mega-super stars like Maria, who have won all four major tournament titles and finished in the Top 10 seven times, but it's just so common because of what I've done. This is really the first time I've said anything about this situation because we're putting it in a book. I don't even talk about it because it's really no big deal. But I guess it could have been a big deal. After going through what I went through with Capriati and then what I went through with the Williamses, this was like, wow, no big deal because we never did go into the contract other than just a rough draft.

In my opinion, there was no doubt she was going to be a great player. She still has her great backhand and great footwork around the ball, but she is still not known for her court mobility, agility and overall athletic ability. But she can hide it because she dictates the point. That forehand is still very, very shaky.

Believe me, if she wouldn't have gotten the help from myself and Robert Lansdorp at a young age she might not have reached the top 30 because of that forehand. I give a lot of credit to the dad for knowing it. And he knew it to the point that he wanted his daughter to play left-handed it was so bad. Now that's having insight.

When you're dealing with high-stakes poker and you're dealing with the top of the line situations with companies like IMG, who have their tentacles every which way, from players to tournaments to TV to network to sponsors, a lot of people in tennis don't realize how huge they are and how they directly and indirectly control the game, but I'm not saying that's bad at all.

In 2000, IMG founder Mark McCormick called me up and I had dinner with him and his wife Betsy Nagelsen in Orlando. He wanted to acquire the rights to my name, he wanted to acquire me. There was discussion about him wanting me to take over the academy part in Bradenton because he saw how I can help position players with the media, and how a young talent gravitates to me, and I could extract greatness. Mark loved how I was put together and my work ethic. I knew right then he was a really smart guy. Ha! We got into serious discussions about a seven-figure acquisition for the rights to my name and so on. They didn't want to purchase the academy because they had already bought the Evert Academy. They were involved with Evert and they had Bollettieri and these things don't work. So he said, "Would you ever entertain coming to Bradenton?" And it took me one second and I said, "No, because I'm my own person. But you could still acquire me!" Even though seven figures could change someone's mind, it never got much farther. There were still some discussions that lingered after that and still do at times. Since then Mark passed away and IMG was sold.

When it's all said and done IMG is the world-wide leader and the best of the best. They not only can open any door, they can make the door. But competitiveness is the name of the game in life and in sports and you're toughest competitor of all time will always be you against you. Please always remember that to extract more greatness. I even attracted more greatness out of IMG as they came sprinting and really stepped up to make Yuri happy! I always say: Fear is the world-wide leader in motivation!

CONNECTING THE DOTS

One of the most common elements that I see in players who have gone on to become great or achieve greatness was 100 percent how they were wired as a competitor. People ask me, "What was the one thing that some of these players had that was a little different?" It wasn't as much the forehand or the backhand or the movement. These are all pieces of the puzzle. The common thread that they all shared is their competitiveness.

Day in and day out, no matter if it was cards, checkers, tennis, first in line to get a drink, it just seemed like their competitiveness at an early age was so unique and off the charts. With every kid who goes into anything, there's some degree of competitiveness. Even at the highest level there's the ultimate competitor.

I saw that in the Williams sisters and Capriati, Roddick, and Sharapova. Even though everybody had their pluses and minuses, or their strengths and weaknesses, the only thing that I can say they had in common was they competed like it was their last breath. I really think above and beyond anything that's always the X factor. And I think any coach who can get their student to become a better competitor, that's what it's all about. At the end of the day, you're a competitor first and a tennis player second.

The first step in most sports — tennis, football, basketball – is the most important. Period. But the first step in life is even more important, to get out of bed with a purpose and a passion. With that kind of first step, you'll always be a step ahead.

9

TOMMY HO

Tommy Ho is a very interesting scenario because a lot of people who read this have never heard of him. People in tennis have heard of him and I'm sure there are a lot of people who have their opinions. But we all know what opinions are like! What happened to this boy is he became the most dominant junior tennis player of all time. By age 15, Tommy had 16 national gold balls and could have had more if he wanted to. In tennis, just as in life, it's not where you start it's where you finish. There was really only one person who really knows, maybe two because Tommy and I talked about why he didn't go on to become Andre Agassi, Michael Chang, Pete Sampras, Jim Courier.

First and foremost, when he came to me as a 9-year-old lefty, he had tremendous hand-eye coordination and he had this forehand that to me looked like a ping pong stroke. When he took it back, I couldn't tell which side of the racquet he was hitting the ball with. I'm thinking, wow, this guy has a severe western grip. It's really complicated and could be kind of tough to return serve switching it that much. So I had him hit some balls. No matter what speed I gave him the ball, he always hit the ball in front of him, whether I gave it to him fast, high, slow or low he always hit it in front of him. He could get the racquet from where it started to where it had to go, which was very uncanny. It was natural. It was spot on every time. It was very rhythmic. It was very connected.

He could find angles with this forehand like I'd never seen. It would look like he'd hit it cross court and it would just drop into the service box like you're throwing it there. And I thought, wow, this is interesting. If he could just learn to flatten the ball out and hit through it, his forehand could be world class.

His dad told me when they went to a camp in 1985 at the late, great Harry Hopman's, he wanted to change him to an eastern grip so he'd hit the ball cleaner and flatter. I said, "Listen, nothing against Harry Hopman (who at the time was one of the greatest coaches ever), but I saw it differently. I think if we moved the grip a little bit to a semi-western it could be scary! With his hands and that racquet speed and what I'm seeing, what everybody thinks is bizarre and unorthodox I see it as a weapon. I've never seen anybody hit at angles like this. I've never seen that racquet speed, no matter if he's nervous or if he's confident. It's a blur. He accelerates. There's no hesitation, there's no delay. The wiring from the brain to the arm never changed. And you can't read it when he hits up the line. So my take is, I wouldn't change it. What everybody thinks is against the grain or out of the box, but being a lefty it was a game-changing stroke. I know the game is getting faster but I wouldn't change it." I saw greatness. Others saw speed bumps.

So, we go down this road and we don't change his forehand grip too much. His return of serve is kind of tough because he has to go a long way with both grips. This kid is really the first who I had who I really wanted to be the best player in the country.

Back in the mid-1980s, I just liked helping anybody, whether it be adults, kids, or a cat! Meow! It was never my goal to have an academy. It was never my goal to want to have someone who was a pro or for me to travel on the pro tour. It wasn't about that. It was more about helping people delivering the service as director of tennis at a resort. It was just about helping others. Even though I had this gift to coach and motivate and educate, it was never like I was on a mission.

This kid's progression went from like No. 48 in Florida in the 12's to the next year being No. 1 in Florida in the 12s, to winning every single national in the United States in singles and doubles to the point where he won a tournament called "Sport Goofy," which was held in Orlando at Disney World and was kind of a world championship. That same year, there was this girl named Monica Seles, who won the girls' tournament. Tommy won the Orange Bowl that year, losing about seven games. He crushed everybody like a grape! Wasn't that grape? Ha!

You can imagine people going to watch the Orange Bowl, which is the best of the best among juniors in the world, and he wins 0 and 0 in the semifinals. He's physically abusing kids with a 110-mile-an-hour left-handed serve, which in itself had kids playing dodge ball. He had a kick serve already at that age that would bounce over people's heads, or they'd swing twice at it. These were the best kids in the world. It was a joke.

More importantly, he just kept the ball going crosscourt. His left-handed forehand to your backhand, five, six, seven, eight in a row until the court was so open like the Red Sea and he would, bingo, rip it down the line. He literally was winning nationals losing eight or 12 games the whole tournament! The only person who had even a kind of battle with him was a kid named Ivan Baron, who was mentally strong and maybe had a shot to be a pro someday too.

It was amazing and I always thought what Tommy was doing was great. Most of all he was an amazing kid. But I never looked at it any farther that he was going to beat Jimmy Connors, John McEnroe or someone like that because he wasn't that athletic. His movement was average. He wasn't a great athlete from the waist down, but from the waist up he was the closest thing swinging a racquet to Rod Laver that anybody has ever seen. It was amazing his racquet speed and his hand-eye coordination with his left hand. Plus he had an incredible ability to focus. He had uncanny concentration for his age. He was a wizard and he lived in Winter Haven and not the Emerald City.

I tell this to people today: If he was playing on Court One and someone got shot on Court Two, he'd continue to play the point and wouldn't look over there. His ability to focus and the maturity he had at a young age to dial in and just laser beam was scary. Tommy had exceptional coaching, very good stroke mechanics, an amazing serve. And he was about 5-foot-10, so he was a little bigger than the other kids. You put that together with a game plan where you don't miss until the court opens, keep it going crosscourt, and you're bigger and more mature, that's a recipe to demolish anybody on the other side of the net. That also gives you the capability to start playing stronger competition.

As this unfolds, he goes into the 14s and he does the same thing. He wins everything. So then I make the leap and say, "Listen, what I want you to do is play in the 18s as a 14-year-old. The same thing as Jennifer Capriati did."

People were against it. The USTA said, "No, he should play Florida Designated tournaments." I said to Tommy, "Listen, you've answered every bell. Let's play the 16s indoors and let's see how you do as a 13 year old."

The kids are bigger, stronger and faster at the 16s indoors and the courts are quicker. What does he do? He wins the title. So he jumps up two age groups. He answers that bell. Ding! Ding!

I say, "Now you can definitely play the 18s." The Easter Bowl comes around the corner at Doral in Miami and he plays the 18s and does well and he finishes third as a 14-year-old. There's MaliVai Washington, Jonathan Stark, Fritz Bissell and Jared Palmer in the field. He finishes third and now he's 15. He not only has what it takes mentally, he has some weapons. He then plays the 18s full time and finishes in the top 10 at the USTA National Hard Court Championships. He plays the Clay Courts and finishes in the top 10. Not bad for a kid 15 years old. Actually, it's unreal.

At the same time, I was working with Jennifer Capriati. So I had this 15-year-old playing the 18s and setting the world on fire and I had this 12-year-old playing the 18s. At the same time, Tommy finished in the top 10 at the Hard Courts, Jennifer won the Hard Courts. Then Jennifer played the Clay Courts two weeks later and she wins and Tommy finishes in the top 10.

Then Tommy went to Kalamazoo, Mich., for the USTA National 18s and he was seeded No. 10. He has three or four "Houdini" escapes and barely beats some people. I see Todd Martin lose 0 and 0 and he went on to be top five in the world, just to show you junior tennis with boys doesn't mean a lot at the end of the day. Tommy ends up beating Martin Blackman 6-4 in the fifth set in the final and wins the tournament. You talk about timing in life, the year before Michael Chang won the tournament and he's Asian-American, and now you've got this other Asian-American winning the next year but he's bigger and stronger and he has a better serve.

This is when the agents or the people who really can't evaluate talent were saying that Tommy was going to be much better than Michael. What I am thinking is "No way, Jose." This Chang kid could stop on a dime, and movement in tennis is like keys to the car. If you can move and can play offense and defense and change direction, you have options. You can dictate or negate when you have that. When you're nervous you can still hang in there. If you're nervous and you're not that fast, see you later alligator. I knew the game was going to get bigger and faster, and was going to be a bigger challenge to return serve, which was always going to be an issue with me with Tommy because of the grips.

He wins Kalamazoo and now you've got ProServ, IMG, Advantage and all the agencies under the sun saying, "We can get you millions, blah, blah, blah." And the dad sits down with me and I say, "Listen, he has to turn pro. If someone is going to offer your son a couple million dollars, if he doesn't make it he has money set aside to go to college for the rest of his life, whatever. He has to do it, it's that simple." But if he wouldn't have played up, none of this probably would have happened. He probably would have gone to college. Timing in life is huge and it can be huge to have great timing, on and off the court!

With Tommy Ho

After Chang, Asian, bigger, stronger but not faster -- that was the sell. And Fila jumped all over it. Nike wanted it. Reebok wanted it. ProKennex wanted it. Wilson wanted it. So Tommy had to turn pro, which none of us were expecting. I knew it was going to blow up because he wasn't going to go out there and start winning matches. I think he lost in the first round in qualifying maybe 15 times in a row. Good losses, but he lost more the first year on the pro tour than he did in five years in junior tennis. And mentally that can take a toll. But it's not where you start, it's where you finish. I had to do more "Macci Magic" and keep Tommy believing and plugged in because he was always losing, and that really affects the big C, as in confidence.

I knew Tommy was never going to be great. I knew he could be good. I thought he could be top 50. I knew he could be a top 10 in the world doubles player because you don't have to cover the whole court. If you've got a good doubles partner you've got a shot. But now since he's the "youngest" everybody is thinking -- sports psychologists, agents, media -- he's almost now the poster child of don't turn pro young, look at what happened to Tommy Ho.

Well, I can set the record straight. Whether he turned pro at 15, 16, went to college for a year at Stanford, he ended up where he ended up because that's how good he was. He got to about No. 80 in the world in singles and No. 7 in doubles. He got to the semifinals of the French Open in doubles. He beat Sergi Bruguera, who was No. 3 in the world. He had a lot of good losses, some good wins. That's kind of where I thought he'd end up because of his movement. But he had other attributes and you've got to have a package, especially in the men's game. The physicality fed into his weaknesses. He had more power and hit faster serves than anyone in the juniors, but because he was not the big man on campus and running the show in the pros like he had in the juniors, it affected his mental toughness.

So when people said it was too much too soon, they were wrong. He was big, that's why he won. Wrong. A lot of people are big and they don't win in the juniors. Could he have done a little better? I think all of us in life could have done a little better. But in so many things, it is timing, the luck of the draw and so on. Plus he had a little scoliosis and he had some elbow problems. But at the end of the day, he over-achieved, in my opinion. When I say that, people look at me and say, what am I talking about? He over-achieved? I never in my wildest dreams thought he would be that good. But when you win Kalamazoo and people give you millions, you're supposed to be the next flavor of the month. That's what makes the world go around and people can look at it. But when you're in the fish bowl and you're in that driver's seat and he's in the passenger seat or vice versa, you see it with a different set of eyes. The most important thing is he's a great kid. He has a great family and he had some of the best hands I've ever seen. He had magician's hands! I guess you could say I've got to hand it to him.

I remember him playing video games back in the day when Pac-Man was the rage. He could go faster using a plastic fork and spoon playing video games and still beat all the kids. His hands were just amazing. Also Tommy was a little bit lazy. I wanted to instill my intensity and my passion and my enthusiasm. I did to some degree, but when I saw him take a jump shot with a basketball and he shot it over the goal and into the bushes, I said, "This is going to be a little rough. I'm glad he's hitting groundstrokes instead of shooting jumpers."

If you really want to talk about how my teaching got started, it's all because of Tommy. There's always a start to everything. A lot of times in life, people don't appreciate or they forget where they have come from and how it started. Tommy Ho is my reason. And through his success, Stefano Capriati thought I could help his daughter, and the list grew on and on.

There might not even be this book right now if it weren't for Tommy because that kind of started this whole thing for people to give me a look, to let me do my thing on a bigger stage or better platform to extract greatness from them with my delivery and my mindset as a coach, teacher and role model. Or people thought maybe this Macci guy knows what's going on and he can help us in so many areas. Tommy's family was the best family -- they were like my family. Tommy was like my son. It was just a great situation. I treated every match that he played like the Super Bowl because that was the beginning. I went to every local tournament and all those up the ladder to every national. I was so engaged in that. It was the passion. I was, believe me, all in for Tommy Ho.

I remember sitting in a Wendy's restaurant in San Diego, California, after he played in Balboa Park and had just finished being the first kid ever to win every singles and every doubles national tournament in an age category. He's eating a hamburger and fries and killing a Frosty and I said, "What do you think about what you just accomplished?" And he said, "What do you mean?" I said, "Never mind, we'll talk about it on the plane." That was Tommy Ho at his finest, humble for sure. But then again maybe he was just locked into that juicy burger and fries. I told you the kid could focus. He just won for the fourth time the national singles and doubles, he won eight gold balls. It was like not a big deal to him. I'm sure he was happy and all that. I guess his success meant more to me, and he really did put Winter Haven, Florida, on the map in tennis. They even had a "Tommy Ho Day" there. He put Grenelefe on the map to some degree too. He put me on a brand new map. He made other juniors run all over the map!

I think a lot of times people forget the beginning because they're so caught up in the moment. That's why it's so important to acknowledge him. Tommy has never changed and he has always appreciated. He still has enormous character and his family has enormous character. Maybe he hadn't had the success of these other people who became No. 1, but if you listen to him speak in front of others, or you listen to Tommy talk as a keynote speaker at a banquet and talk about life and hard work and just how his life and career evolved, it comes across loud and clear what Rick Macci did for him -- the qualities that were instilled in him that maybe he didn't realize. He's proud to acknowledge how I extracted greatness like he never knew he had inside.

Where maybe others who become bigger than life (they think) or they become bigger than the rest of it, most all the recognition is going to stay in the family, not to a coach or others who have helped them. That's unfortunate but that's OK. That's what makes the world go around. Tommy is the same great human being today that he was at nine years old. The subplot: Even today I teach his kids when they come to Florida. How cool is that? It means two things: He wants me to influence his kids as I did him. And, secondly, I'm older. Ouch!

When I talk about that beginning, it was by far the most enjoyable time in my career because it was new and it was exciting and it was the first. And I was on a mission to make this kid the best he could be. Through his success, other people thought I might be kind of smart and kids are saying, "Can you come and teach me? Can we stay with you and live with you?" I said, "Wait a minute, I don't want anybody living with me other than my cat." Meow. Then I started the academy and it just kind of took a life of its own. You learn as you go to make it bigger or smaller.

And believe me, when he won the lottery, when he got millions in endorsements because of winning Kalamazoo, we didn't have a contract. Even though his parents paid for everything, when he came into major endorsements they were very appreciative of what I did or tried to do for their son Tommy. It was just a lot more than tennis. The whole family is just class people.

10

MARY PIERCE

I first saw Mary Pierce play tennis when she was 12 years old; she had very good compact strokes. The forehand and backhand were very solid and she was going to be a strong girl, so I knew off the ground she would have firepower when she went onto the pro tour. Her athletic ability was OK. It wasn't off the charts but it wasn't going to be a detriment. Her serve could be developed.

This probably was when she was about age 15, when I was in Delray Beach and Venus and Serena were 11 and 12. The Pierces decided to leave IMG Academy because they felt they weren't getting enough attention. I talked to Mary's father, Jim, and worked out an arrangement where I got them a place to live and she could train at the academy and I'd give her a hitting partner. And we'd eventually work a deal out so I could help her more and more and she could play out of the academy.

She was just starting to dabble on the pro tour at 16 years old, playing some $25,000 tournaments and some $50,000 tournaments. What I really liked about Mary was the power she possessed. She didn't back up at all. She took the ball early. Her groundstrokes were very compact on both sides. Basically, she just hit the crap out of the ball! Full throttle! I guess you could say piercing, but I won't say that.

But it was very obvious to me that Jim was very controlling and it was him really living through his daughter. The mom hardly said a word and Mary didn't have a lot to say and brother David was quite young at the time, so he was just kind of there at the academy hitting balls. It was really Jim and he'd do some drills with her. I remember a drill called the Colombian Suicide Drill in which he'd throw balls to her. I have no idea what the benefit of this was but it made him feel good. But Jim is a good guy. He wanted to be in control like most of the fathers but he couldn't hit the ball and really didn't have the idea of the technical part or strategic part. Yet like most of these fathers they want the credit and that was fine. I just wanted to help her and she was a great girl. But even when she was 16 years old, I knew she wasn't going to be a Venus or Serena Williams, even though they were only 11 and 10 and little kids. No one thought that Venus and Serena were good at a young age, they just saw mistakes and they just saw what they wanted to see. Remember there is an art to really evaluating talent and few possess that vision and can feel the future.

Mary Pierce

Nothing was going to make me take the eye off the ball with Venus and Serena even though I had this girl, who is 16 years old and she's starting to beat people ranked No. 80, 90, 100 in the world. I was having a coach from the academy go with her to tournaments, so we were really trying to help her in this situation. Whenever I had a chance, I'd spend time with her and work with her. But I provided, more importantly, the environment because I was spending so much time with the Williams girls.

Then when we wanted to enter into a contract -- I'll never forget this -- Jim went to IMG and they prepared a contract and in the contract it said if I want to say anything to Mary I have to tell Jim first, then he would tell Mary. And I said, "You've got to be kidding me." I don't even think I read the rest of it. I just crumbled it up and shot a 10-foot jump shot into the trash can (made it. Basketball days, Greenville, Ohio) and said, "You can practice here and whatever you want to do is fine" because obviously he wanted control of the situation and I just didn't need that type of situation. I wanted to help everybody and, more importantly, my main focus was Venus and Serena. If I was going to go really above and beyond something I didn't need to deal with that. We just helped them out.

And then I said to Jim, "Since we're not going to do the deal you've got to take care of your own condo. You're daughter is starting make some money now." That didn't sit too well with him. He got a little upset with that one. But that's the way it is.

I remember one day, a bit later on, I was waiting for her on the court at 7 in the morning in Delray. They were staying on the fifth floor at the old Laver's tennis resort where they have these high-rise condos and I hear an argument up there. All of a sudden I see clothes flying through the air like kites as the hitting partner and I are waiting down below on the court. I guess there was some argument or something and it was just kind of interesting to see all this stuff flying down. Fifteen minutes later Mary comes down and she feels badly and apologizes and gives me a note apologizing. She was embarrassed about what happened. She was such a sweet kid but very mentally strong. I really admired that quality. I feel I probably helped instill that attribute and it helped make Mary a better player.

I told Jim, "Listen, I know you've driven a lot of stuff into her but you don't want to drive her away from you because at 18 you never know what's going to happen." Lo and behold at 18 years old the whole thing took a wrong turn and she didn't want him around. That was unfortunate because Jim's a good guy and I like him and it was more about him and a strong ego.

Jim did a great job getting her to where she got to. She won the French Open in 2000 and the Australian Open in 2005 and was ranked as high as No. 3 in 1995. As far as pure striking of the ball, the forehand and the backhand, Jennifer Capriati is No. 1 and Mary Pierce is No. 1-A. Mary was right behind her. I've seen her take Steffi Graf and a lot of people to the woodshed playing right through them. You talk about someone who could just annihilate you with just raw power. Even on clay Mary could do that. When she's fearless and she's on a mission, you talk about someone who could just play through someone with relentless power. Wow!

It wasn't a long relationship with Mary, even though Jim stayed there for four or five years. But Mary was an awesome kid and deserved whatever came her way. I think if she'd had a little more in-depth coaching and a little better athleticism and really learned how to change the pace and slice the ball, coupled with that power, she could have played up even another level. She had a great career and just like Jennifer Capriati, she could overwhelm anybody if she was confident. Because she was rock solid on both the forehand and backhand side and because she took the ball early, she going to be able to dictate matches on her terms. When you play someone like that you've got to be careful because they could beat anybody, anytime, anywhere. But if you're not dialed in, it could be trouble and sometimes Mary's phone was not working!

Looking back on working with her and helping her, even though she was a pro and I felt she had Top 10 written all over her, I knew these two younger warriors from Compton, Calif., could transcend the game. So my loyalty or my true dedication, if I was going to have to go above and beyond the call of duty, was always going to be with Venus and Serena.

11

ANASTASIA MYSKINA

When Anastasia Myskina was 17 she played the Orange Bowl tournament and was the third best of the Russians. Nadia Petrova and Elena Dementieva were better. She was probably the one out of all of them the Russian Tennis Federation didn't think that much of simply because her forehand was very, very flat and her serve almost didn't even register on the radar gun. They probably saw what they wanted to see, but she didn't have the high-powered results of the others, such as winning major junior titles.

At the time, I was coaching a lot of players, including one Russian named Katia Afinoginova, whose brother Maxim played for the Buffalo Sabres hockey team. He was the No. 1 junior hockey player in the world and through that relationship, his agent Mark Gandler wanted to get involved with some tennis players. One thing led to another because he had this Russian connection and there was this introduction to Anastasia and her father. Plus I saw her play at the Orange Bowl and I saw some things that I thought had a lot of potential. I thought she could move way above average. I thought she had a world-class backhand and mentally I thought that she had something. You can get away with hitting a flat forehand in the women's game, but in men's tennis, you've got to grab it more and play with more spin. Her forehand wasn't that much of a liability.

We did a contract and represented her to have a percentage of endorsements and prize money and we would train her. She immediately turned pro and made a meteoric rise the first year. She went from No. 293 to No. 65 in 1999. She might have squirted through there faster than anybody other than when Serena made her splash.

I took her to the U.S. Open to play, where she won three matches to qualify, and in the first round she had to play Mary Joe Fernandez, who was seeded. They had similar games except obviously one has more experience and had been ranked in top 10 in the world. I knew Anastasia had a legitimate shot to win.

The moral of the story -- here's the qualifier getting through and playing Fernandez and was serving for the match at 5-4 in the third and she ended up losing 7-5. Right then I knew there was no doubt Anastasia could be top 10 in the world because of the way she covered the court, plus she was not afraid to pull the trigger. Her backhand down the line was money and with the flat ball off the forehand, she could hit through the ball. It wasn't really a liability. Her second serve clocked in the high 50s, which was ridiculously slow. However, she had enough makeup speed that if someone tatooed a return, she could play defense and kind of get back in the point. Her serve was something that definitely needed to be addressed. She'd hit it and back way up and go into the prevent defense. It was more of a courage thing, not being afraid thing, than it was technical because it was a smooth stroke. She'd hit it and back up and was ready to scamper.

As the year went on and she got a boyfriend and the dad starts to get more involved and I am thinking "Here we go. Trouble. Deja vu all over again." They want out of the contract we have and the boyfriend is traveling with us now and the deal becomes lopsided. I don't know how much money was made off of that but the big money was going to be made down the road. You don't do this to get someone to No. 80 in the world. The big money is if you win the French Open, which is what she ended up doing in 2004. The big money is when you get the endorsements.

Her dad was a good guy and she was an amazing kid. I really enjoyed working with her, but it was a little different situation for me. She was 17, 18, 19 years old, whereas a lot of times I'm taking the kid when they're 9 until they're 16. It was different because a lot of the dirty work that I usually do was already done. This was more tactics and strategy and motivation and just trying to tweak whatever could be tweaked. So it was the right situation.

Anastasia Myskina

I knew that she could be one of the best players in the world and she got all the way to No. 2 in the world in 2004. But people forget that she won the French Open. She was right in there. She was a tough out. She could run and she could fight and she had groundstrokes that were solid. The backhand was like a Capriati or Pierce, the forehand was a cut below but she moved better than both of them. She's was a great athlete. She played low to the ground and that's a good recipe in women's tennis. You don't have to volley that much. You don't have to have a big serve or the touch and feel. That's more like the appetizer. She had the main course and she had those groundstrokes. I knew it at a young age even though she was not one of the better Russians. She hit flat Russian rockets!

Once again it comes down to the ability to evaluate talent and no one is psychic and no one has a crystal ball. I've been wrong. No one is always right, but I've been right a heck of a lot more than wrong about greatness. You've also got to have the passion and the energy to dig deep to help extract greatness and connect the dots to help others.

Anastasia was a super polite girl and had a very nice family, but as these things play out it's very hard to keep your hands around it. What we did for her and the improvement she had when she was at the academy and working with her was phenomenal. The success she had was well deserved, and she'll always be one of my favorites because she was so appreciative and respectful.

12

MONIQUE VIELE / DONALD TRUMP

I've been fortunate to be around a lot of great athletes in every sport and know why they become very marketable. People have to understand a lot of times companies and manufacturers do things on your ability or your potential. They try to project and they want to get that relationship with you early on. You've either got to be very successful in the juniors or do something way out of the box so that they see a lot of potential.

Some of these kids who have played up in their age groups and had success give you a little bit of a snapshot. It's a feeling of, okay, I think they have a chance to do well in the pros or be one of the best juniors in the United States or the world, and that can give other people an idea. But when it's all said and done there's no crystal ball and there's no guarantee.

Monique Viele

Yet a player like Venus gets a $12 million deal, $2.5 million a year from Reebok at age 15 and she only has to play three tournaments a year. People hear that and they think there's all this money in tennis. Unfortunately, it's all at the top or it's all on your ability to be able to bring awareness to someone's brand or to push product. And hopefully you can play!

In Venus's situation, because she was African-American and no one could move like her, Reebok saw an opportunity just like Nike to really form something to take their brand to another level. The same with Serena initially with Puma and then with Nike. The same thing with Sharapova and Nike, and with Roddick when he was with Reebok and later with Lacoste. People have to understand most of this money is at the top. Companies would have to see potential on and off the court if possible.

There are sometimes situations where even if you haven't really proven yourself, if companies think you're marketable or you have crossover capabilities where you can go from the sports page to the front page, or if you can go from the tennis part to Madison Avenue, if they see that capability, even if you're not one of the best players in the world like an Anna Kournikova, the endorsements are there.

A very unique situation that I was involved in during the late 1990s and early 2000s was with a young lady named Monique Viele. She was a pretty good athlete who had good groundstrokes, a 113-mile-an-hour serve to boot. It was really interesting because at age 13 she won the Florida Open junior tournament and she beat the girl who ended up winning the U.S. Open junior title. For Monique, that was really her calling card as a 13-year-old -- she beat one of the best juniors in the world. Other than that, she just played junior tournaments.

So she never did a lot but I think people were looking for something in the U.S. because after the Williams sisters, no one really was coming up. Now, you had this girl who had a lot of ability and hit the ball decently. Her potential was echoed by all the companies that came to the academy to see her play. Bud Collins even quipped that she was the eighth wonder of the world. Nick Bollettieri said she can't miss. So there were a lot of other people who saw her potential.

I questioned her mental toughness a bit because I didn't know how she was wired, but everything else looked as though she could go on to have at least at top 20 career. What was unique about Monique was she modeled, she sang and she danced. So she had more star crossover capabilities to maybe play in a tournament, win it and sing the National Anthem. There was something she could bring to the table that was different than anybody else, and that was echoed in the media.

Fortunately or unfortunately when people feel when you have this ability, it kind of takes a life on its own. The story of her ability spread like wildfire, not just in this country but globally as well. At the end of the day, I let people make their own choice if they're going to write the article or not because she hadn't proven herself yet. Just like Venus hadn't proven herself yet. Some of these kids who are very good still have a lot of questions that have yet to be answered. It happens to many, many kids who never did anything in the pros in any sport.

So this isn't uncommon, but where Monique had layer after layer, she had the same coach as the Williams sisters and Capriati with a different spin now. She left IMG and the father, Rick, wanted me to not only coach her, he wanted me to represent her and negotiate the deals. Maybe he thought I could put more helium in the balloon to market her, but he also wanted her to do something different.

I knew that Donald Trump had a management company called T Management and they represent models and singers and I wondered if they'd be interested in representing someone who could model and sing, and by the way she hits a good tennis ball. I knew Donald had a box at the U.S. Open and he always was involved in tennis.

So I contacted the head pro there at his Mar-a-Lago club up at Palm Beach and he said, "What you want to do Rick is this: You come down Saturday. Donald will come from the house. He'll come to the tennis complex and walk through the complex and he goes out and plays 18 holes of golf. And this will be about 9:30." So, this is exactly what I do. We're there practicing on Court One by the clubhouse and Monique is hitting balls with the hitting partner from the academy. The Trumpster knows nothing about it. He walks up and he's used to seeing his members there or people who aren't really that good. Now, he's seeing this girl out there, 5-8 and 110 pounds, just blistering groundstrokes off both sides. He walks up and asks Anthony, "Who's that?" And Anthony says, "There's Rick Macci, her coach. Let me introduce you." They come and make the introduction and I'm having this conversation with Donald and I kind of filled him in and told him a little bit about the background and where we're at. I said, "I think there's some endorsement opportunities and she just left IMG, maybe there's a possibility. I know you guys do some modeling and singing and acting with T Management, maybe there could be this synergy that we could do something together."

And Donald said, "Well, I know she's a heck of a lot better than the other people who play here, and she looks a hell of a lot better too!"

I said, "You're right about that." He said, "If you need my help, give me a call." And off he went to fire 18 holes or to fire someone. Ha!

So the seed was planted. Later he told me, "Rick, she hits the ball just as well as anybody I see at the Open." I said, "You're right, she does hit the ball that well, but hitting the ball and playing are two different things. There's a difference between a hitter and a player and she's 14 and it's going to take time, but there's some endorsement opportunities here. The singing and the modeling are very important to her and her family, too."

He said, "Like I said earlier, if there's anything I can do, let me know."

A week passed, her dad and I talked about it. I got a hold of the head pro again and he gave me the name of the general counsel, Donald's attorney. So Rick Viele and I flew to New York to meet with Bernie Diamond, who was general counsel for the Trump Organization. We go to Trump Towers and negotiate the arrangement that I'm going to be a consultant for T Management and they do all the contractual part of the deals. And they're going to get her opportunities to get in teen magazines and sing National Anthems and start doing some modeling and get some stories other than tennis. I'll handle the tennis and they'll handle the other.

We do the deal and everything is full steam ahead. After it's all done we go into Donald's office and Bernie says, "Everything's done. We're going to represent Monique and Rick's going to run the tennis." Donald says, "Great. You're the best!" I come to find out he says that a lot. It's Friday and he says, "When are you going back to Florida?" I said, "We've got a flight at 6." He said, "My plane leaves at 4. Why don't you guys come back with me?" We decided, alright, since we're done early we'll go back with the Trumpster!

We went on Donald's private plane and it's full of a cast of characters, to say the least. Donald and his new wife, Melina, and his ex-wife, Ivana, are on the plane. There are some CEOs who are coming from New York down to Mar-A-Lago to vacation because there's a spa there. And Donald is just one of the guys, just talking, and nicest guy that you'd ever want to meet and I thought pretty much down to earth. A lot of people probably see him on TV as some guy who's super wealthy or whatever, but he's one of the guys who was in real estate and knew how to market. That's how I look at it. Plus he is smarter than smart.

Through that relationship and talking to him the whole time about tennis, I realize he's a real sports nut. He owned the New Jersey Generals of the former U.S Football League. He's just a really good guy, period. I've been fortunate to be around a lot of people and to me he's just one of the guys, even though he is looked at much differently. I feel he is brilliant and he knows how to play the game of life.

On the plane, there was the CEO of *Shape* magazine. He was a good player, ranked in the east and about 45 years old. Donald said, "Rick, who do you think would win, 14-year-old Monique or this guy who's the best 45-year-old in the east?" I said, "I've never seen him play but I'll bet $1,000 Monique would kick his butt." And Donald said, "You've got it. We're betting on Monique. The match is on. Let's tee it up." Show time!

It turned out it was the next day, and we go there at 9 o'clock to Mar-A-Lago and Donald comes at the same time. He always has these five or six people following him, they call them his tail, I guess, and they follow him everywhere. People are really anticipating this match and there is betting going on all over the place. One hundred dollar bills are flying everywhere.

Donald comes up to me and says, "Are you sure that she's going to win?" I said, "There's no doubt in my mind. You better be right! Like you in real estate I'm seldom wrong" He said, "There's no doubt in Rick's mind and I'm giving you three to one." Everybody's taking the guy and nobody is betting on Monique. Donald said with an authoritative tone that I never heard before, "Hey, pal, you better be right. The Trumpster doesn't lose." I hoped so too because I just went from "the best" to "hey, pal."

They actually have a pretty close match but Monique wins. It was never really in doubt. So Donald is going around collecting and saying, "Never bet against the Trumpster. The Trumpster knows tennis." A lot of bravado. He was very proud. It was like even though it was something you would think is very microscopic and so basic in his world that he deals in, I think whatever is in front of him it shows you how competitive he is. He's saying, "I'm right about this, too" to his billionaire friends who were watching. The guy loves to win. The guy has to win. The guy will find a way to win. It's in the Trump wiring. The guy is just a winner.

It was kind of funny and Monique's stock went up in his eyes and mine did too as he would start saying, "Rick's the best. Rick's the best" whenever someone is around. At least I lost the "hey, pal" label. Yea!

So the next week they want to make another bet with this guy playing Monique's hitting partner, who at the time was No. 170 in the world. That's a pretty darn good hitting partner. And I bet the guy wouldn't get more than four games. Everybody jumped on the bet that this guy would get more than four games for sure. The bets were flying, hundreds of dollar bills on this bet. I told Bo, the hitting partner, "I not only want you to beat him, I don't want you to take any chances. I just want you to keep it going and I want you to run the guy. Just keep running him and running him and torture him. And if you don't let him get a game I'll give you half of the bet. So you're out here playing an hour and a half and could win $300." To Bo, that was like $3,000.

I told Donald, "You should up the ante. You should take it as far as he won't get more than a game a set." I saw how the guy served and he wasn't going to get aces on Bo. Once the point started, on clay, against a guy No. 170 and he's a guy who's ranked No. 1 in the east in the 45's? Good night. It ain't gonna happen. Game, set, match. Bo!

Bo wins the first set is 6-0 and is up 3-0 in the second and the guy has to retire. They have to call paramedics (I'm serious) because the guy is cramping. He has a full body cramp from the neck to the calf. Lucky that Mar-A-Lago has a spa. The guy is in the spa all day getting put back together like the scarecrow in the Wizard of Oz. He really needed rewiring physically and mentally. Donald wins hundreds if not thousands on the bet and he's going around again saying, "Never bet against the Trumpster. I know tennis." It was the funniest thing because it was like the most important thing to him. And you know what it does? He just lasers in on one thing -- big or small -- and makes it like the Super Bowl. That is why he is so successful.

So while T Management is working to get Monique some off-court opportunities, I'm in the negotiations with racquet companies and some clothing companies, mainly Fila and Nike, because Nike with the crossover appeal and Monique being athletic and all the things that she could do, how they could use that. I remember Nike's head of international promotions said, "You should come and work for us. This portfolio you put together of her dunking a basketball and serving a volleyball and on a skateboard is awesome."

I put a presentation of her capabilities as an athlete, while showcasing her obvious good looks. I knew Viele is an Italian name and Fila is out of Italy. Since I'm good friends with Fila's international promotional executive Marty Mulligan, I go to them first. They all saw her play and saw the other off-court things and what publicity it was generating, so at the U.S. Open I had these back and forth discussions.

One time, I'm with Nike and then Fila and then Nike and then Fila. I said, "We're going to be doing the deal tonight." We met the people from Italy that night at 11:30 in a hallway and wrote it on a napkin. Bernard Diamond and I agreed in principle to terms of the contract for Monique. It was guaranteed $1.8 million for three years, $600,000 a year....and she was

15 years old! Before she ever hit a ball on the pro tour she got one of the biggest endorsement deals ever. Then she got a six-figure racquet deal with Yonex. The next day I met with Donald at his office and once again his line "Rick's the best!" comes out. It should, I just made him $180,000!

So the stage was set for her to be able to travel and play and have the money to do that. She was going to make her debut in Japan. I got her a wild card into the Princess Cup. I thought she would do well. She was having many people follow her at the tournament. People saw a lot of potential or there was a lot of hype and publicity about her. And I didn't know what was going to happen other than she had good groundstrokes and she could hang with girls in the top 100 and her serve was good.

She goes out there and I'm totally blown away how she just freaked out. At 3-all in the first set she just got paralyzed, couldn't run, couldn't hit, made errors. She bounced the ball three times on her serve. One time she bounced it 18 times. She was hyperventilating and she got a delay-of-game warning. And I'm thinking, what the heck? I said right then and there she ain't wired like Venus or Serena or Jennifer. She might have some juice and fire power but mentally there are some things that are going to take awhile, if ever!

She comes back to the United States and she has to play some $25,000, $50,000 and $75,000 lower-level events and she's losing matches, winning matches, getting her ranking into the 300s. And then out of nowhere her father, who was a very good friend of mine, who's Mr. Health and Nutrition, who never drinks soda, never eats certain meats, drinks so much water, is fit as a fiddle, is always telling me, "Why are you drinking that Coke? Don't do that, you should be doing this." Then out of nowhere, he gets sick. He has cancer.

He'd always been against the medical profession, so he does this holistic approach to try to combat it. He does this for three months, which is the wrong thing to do. And by the time he goes to a regular doctor, half his stomach is gone. Many months later, he died. He was 225 pounds, made of steel, and in six months he died. He was 47 years old.

It was so rattling to Monique and her whole family, as it would be to anybody. But this was a very unique situation because Rick Viele was a very controlling, dominant parent. Sound familiar? Even more than a Richard Williams or a Jim Pierce or a Stefano Capriati. I wouldn't say he was a dictator but he very much controlled every move from A to V, as in Viele.

How that affected his daughter was traumatic. She didn't want to play anymore. She didn't have the desire to play. She lost motivation and when she tried to come back she didn't want to come back. Plus she had wrist surgery and the whole thing got lopsided and just blew up.

It was sad because no doubt she could have been a top 50 player, guaranteed. It would have taken some time. She had groundstrokes that were solid and she had a great serve. I think the mental part you learn last and she just didn't have that at a young age. And the hype and publicity superceded the talent, no doubt. But it was the same thing with the Williamses, it's just that they went on to prove it and more.

Monique had so much more greatness to extract inside of her as a tennis player, but the main extractor (her father's situation) changed the road map in her career and her life.

13

MACCISMS

So much of learning and communicating with others is how you present it and how you say things. It's like marketing -- it's the same thing but wrapped differently. It's the same perfume but in a different bottle, or it's the same thing but in a different box. Your words are powerful. Your tone of voice is big time and your body language sometimes speaks louder than words.

I'm not inventing or reinventing the game of tennis or motivation but everybody has told me since I was a kid that I always was able to speak in a unique way with a lot of analogies. There was some vision there and some catchiness to it. Plus word associations and a play off words.

There was always a different way to say something or connect the dots or try to move the needle. Here's a perfect example: If someone didn't hustle for a ball, instead of saying, "You've got to run for every ball," I would say "How good do you want to be?" And they'd tell me. I'd say, "Do you want to be good or great?" And they'd say, "Great." I'd say, "Let me tell you something. Every player in the world will run for that ball like a German shepherd is chasing them. So the next time that ball is wide you've got to get that ball." So we said the same thing but there are two different ways to go about it.

Say someone has an easy volley and someone says "Attack the volley." I might say, "When you have an easy volley like that, I want you to remember one thing: When it's slow, go." So what they'll remember is the word association. When they see the ball slow, they're going to go. They react with their feet then they will attack. They're going to learn quicker through a rhyme or an association. It sticks in their computer better!

Whether it's one word or it's a play on words, or something that just gets your brain thinking, I've always been intrigued to communicate like that. And that is the number one staple of my teaching, period: The art of communication with passion. I try to take the temperature and explain it in a way that just connects. And how you connect it is different with each player. It is not one size fits all.

As time went on, thousands of people, including many CEO's of major corporations, have said to me when they've heard me teach or I've taught them, "Why don't you write a book just on your terminology in the way you explain things?" I said I would someday. Well, I guess today is that day.

They say it's very motivating and crystal clear. I've heard that many times. Through that, I said I have a certain unique lingo that has come to become known as "Maccisims." It's not that I'm saying anything different that billions of people before me haven't said. It's just that how I say it, when I say it, why I say it is the difference. And that's connecting with another person whom I'm dialed in with.

That's really what this is all about, having that feeling, the art of feeling the temperature of "OK, I'm going to say this now." This is the right time to say this now to get the most out of the person and make the most sense. And you're taking cues off of your student. Do they need this? Do they need that? It's just constant probing and measuring the person. OK, here's what they need, here's where I go. I've got to do this. I can see this is a little off.

That's how I go about finding out what to do, then how I say it. I say it in a way where it makes sense or makes people think. It makes people smile or it gives them a pep in their step. I can always tell if they are plugged in by the look in their eyes or body language. I can read the tea leaves. I just feel you can present everything with a positive tone, even if it is constructive criticism. Even if you're negative, there's a way to say it. I'm just a firm believer in this and I just get right to the bottom line and say: "Do you think Roger Federer would do that?" The answer they're going to say is, "No." I'm saying, "OK, do you think with that effort and that attitude I can call the coach at one of the Ivy League schools and say that you're going to go to for four years and be there with nine other guys and they're going to be married to you for four years? They want someone like that on their team?" At least I can get a better effort that day. That is why I take one day at a time and make the next day better.

Instead of me maybe saying "You're lazy" I might say "Have you ever thought of playing golf?" But we will laugh after I say that. That is the art of communication. This is in my wheelhouse and it's really the cornerstone of the way I go about doing everything. People remember my "Maccisms." They print them off and they're hanging in bedrooms around the country. People probably erase my name and put their name on them, I don't know! That is the best compliment when others use your stuff. They came about because it's just the way I try to push the buttons to fire people up. And it's always centered on enthusiasm, passion and a positive attitude, a winning attitude and never say die. Remember, persistence is always undefeated.

Looking at the old theory -- is the glass half empty or half full? How are we going to look at this when you fail? That should make you happy because that's how you've got a chance now to succeed. That's how I want people to look at things. When you miss that forehand into the net, that's great. When you fail, now you can succeed. The more you fail, the more you will succeed because you're trying. Not trying is really failing! I will say, "Now look at how much better you're going to get from that mistake," instead of saying, "You've hit five in a row in the net and getting mad and losing confidence." There's a better way to do digest it. Trust me. Forgetting is the most special skill in life! Except your wife's birthday. Ouch! Or when someone misses a shot and they went for the shot with conviction and passion and they knew they could make it and they missed it by a foot. Instead of saying, "That was low percentage, you should have hit it cross court," I'll say, "That was a great miss. Great courage. If you think you can make it, keep doing it." Believing is magic. Belief is an X factor! Instill that in every person, it's a life changer.

Who is Rick Macci, or any other coach, to tell anybody how they're really feeling inside? We don't know what they're really feeling. And you don't know what they're going to be feeling when they're 6, 8, 12, 14, 16, 18 years old. Why do you want to put fear in a child? Why do you want to put doubt? Why do you want to put indecision?

Because let's face it, in life when people get confidence, they feel they can do anything. So building the big "C" in people is gigantic and that's been one of the springboards in my teaching and in these Maccisms that has triggered many people to not only go on to become some of the best players in the world but to be the best they can be. They've maxed out their ability because I get them to believe before they have any chance to think about believing.

The power of words and how you deliver them as a teacher is a game of life changer for anybody on your radar.

It's all about the communication. When people read these Maccisms, such as: "A winner finds a way" or "Never make excuses" or "Keep popping the popcorn (keep moving your feet)" or "Extra butter (that means you've really got to move your feet)" they can relate to those things. More importantly they remember them because they're catchy, unique and stick! And from Rick!

When I say to a young student, "OK, you need to become a better competitor," I could say it that way or I could say: "You need a brain, you need a heart and you need courage. And you don't have to see the Wizard to get these. These are key ingredients because the mind controls the body. What I want you to do is work on these qualities." Or when they see stuff like that written it radiates. They're looking over there and seeing the sign: "Enjoy the battle." That's what it's all about, because at the end of the day it's all about you competing. You don't have control over winning and losing. You have control over your best effort, doing the best you can, and winning is going to be a byproduct of that. I want the kids to enjoy the competition. The No. 1 goal is to get them to be the best competitor they can be. That is being a great coach, getting someone to compete better! They are a competitor first, a tennis player second! This is true in any sport, remember that.

It's not the best forehand or backhand, even though all that stuff is big time. But if I can get them to be the best competitor then they're going to handle pressure and they'll play the best they can. It has been proven, not only in business but in sports, the best players have the best attitudes. Tiger Woods and Michael Jordan don't go out there and make excuses. Even in the media room when a reporter says to Woods, "Oh, you missed 16 of 18 fairways, you're game is in a slump. What's going on?" Woods says, "Yeah but I one-putted 14 greens and I'm playing great." He doesn't even want people in the media getting any negativity in his little hemisphere. That is true greatness. Period. Even if he was sick, he looked at it as a challenge, not a liability.

You go back through time and you look at Jordan. I'm talking the ultimate, the best basketball player in the world. He would never make excuses! Never! It was always flipped in his mind as a challenge, period. If he had a sore throat, that's alright, he was going to use his feet anyway. It is a choice, period. Choose positive! Trust me! Also, if you booed him, he loved being booed.

They look at those things as challenges. You've got to flip it in your mind. And that's what greatness does. When someone is facing a sand trap and another sand trap and water and more water, the great ones are picking out a spot right next to the hole and they're going to picture it. And the other guy is going to say, "I hope I don't hit it in the water." And you know what's going to happen. Most likely he will visit the beach or the ocean real soon!

The Maccisms are about attitude, trying to get a hold of someone's attitude, getting them to think a certain way. That's going to trickle down or ripple your mental toughness, and once again it's going to radiate not only to your tennis game but in the game of life.

When I see people change their attitude because of the influence of the Maccisms, it's huge because that's one thing you've got control over. You've got control over how you think. It is a choice! Plain and simple. It is really a choice.

Everything around you could influence you, or something in the past could influence you. You don't have control over the past and you really don't have control over the future, but you have control over how you're going to feel and respond to things right now, and that will or could affect the future. You've got to stay in the moment. Embrace it. Each day is a blessing. Get better every day, and it starts with attitude.

Here is another: If someone gives you a bad call, you can take a deep breath and move to the other side, or you can go crazy and let it bother you. It is a choice. I know people who are still complaining about things 20 years later. That's rough because life's too short. Way too short! Plus, with that negative attitude if you keep complaining guess what you get better at? Complaining!

And I get into these things with kids when I talk to them on the court. There are many motivational signs out there, and it's another way of reaching out, sharing my thoughts and views which are proven through time. That's not because I've had people reach No. 1 in the world. That has nothing to do with it. It really is about how I know how it has changed people's outlook and how it's not only helped them as a tennis player but influenced them as to how they try to go about doing things. Remember, it is really just a choice. But if the Maccism can help extract greatness and rewire a few circuits, I have delivered what I'm here on earth to do -- to help others.

Now whether they can sustain all the pressures that come at you in life and keep that, I don't know. But through these Maccisms, I've given them a little more glue, a little more belief and confidence to handle things that come their way. Because when something happens, you've got to make a decision, and you're going to respond negatively or positively. You have a choice!

That's what I feel I was put here to do -- make a difference in people's lives, to teach people, to mold people, to influence people. That gives me the most satisfaction. That's my gift. It just happens to be that I teach tennis. I know an amazing amount about strokes and strategies but I know a lot more about how to communicate and extract greatness. And through these Maccisms, it's been a big conduit for all ages and all levels that even if they don't have interaction with me I've hopefully been able to help them. Even if it's one little thing in their life, that's a great feeling. Remember things are only unthinkable if you think they are unthinkable! Think about that!

<u>THE MACCISMS</u>

It is a great sign if you read all these Macci signs.

Believing is magic.

Laziness is the X factor that destroys talent.

Confidence is the most powerful weapon. Make sure it's your best friend ever.

It's OK to be nervous. Don't ever be afraid.

To achieve greatness it starts with responsibility.

Be ready so you don't have to get ready.

There's not a wrong way or a right way. There's a better way.

Players who quit get better at quitting.

Players who say "I can't" won't.

You control the situation. Don't let the situation control you.

Players who are lazy get better at becoming lazy.

Players who make excuses get better at making excuses.

Rule #1: Run for every ball. Rule #2: See rule #1

Tennis is a game of inches. It's from one ear to another.

To get the real edge, practice on your day off.

He who hesitates loses.

The difference between ordinary and extraordinary is the little extra.

Having the ability to forget is the real key to mental toughness.

The past is the past, today is today.

Players with great attitudes don't lose, they learn.

Winners find a way, losers find an excuse.

A smart coach or player is smart because he knows he's not that smart.

Love the battle. That is a real competitor.

You only have control over right now.

The strong get stronger, the weak get weaker.

If you run for every ball, you're sending a message.

Well done is a lot better than well said.

Fear is an illusion.

The blame game is a game all losers play. Just compete and shut up.

It is easy to get really upset, so stay positive to avoid the real upset.

The mind is the ultimate weapon. Make sure you don't use it on yourself.

If you have an unreal work ethic, that is only a start.

Would have, should have, could have. Please just get the job done.

Intensity -- you can feel it in the air.

Let it happen -- not make it happen.

One athlete with courage makes a majority.

Breathe out when you hit and you'll be a breath of fresh air.

Step up or get stepped on.

If you reach the head of the mountain top, find another one. Two heads are better than one.

If you play the out balls, the ones in are a piece of cake.

You've got to remember, but you also have to forget.

Nothing comes from nothing.

A good coach improves your game. A great coach improves your life.

When the world is against you, that is when greatness is discovered.

If there is no risk, there are no titles.

It is easy to be good when things are good. I want you to be good when things are bad.

Don't get mad, get more determined.

If you never make excuses, your mind will grow stronger.

Real determination is running over broken glass to get to the ball.

Real, real determination is running over broken glass to get to the ball, then back over it to get the next one.

Train your mind every day to be positive.

If you make a mistake and you don't correct it, you just made another one.

If you think something is impossible, it is for you.

See it, feel it, smell it, touch it, do it.

When the going gets tough, you should have been tougher earlier.

There's a huge difference between a great hitter and a great player.

Your mind is more powerful than any nuclear weapon because a mind built the weapon.

There's a big difference between inspiration and desperation.

Players that make excuses are like the number one. They always have one.

If you wake up each morning, that alone should make you feel great.

Some coaches prefer stressing deep knee bends. I prefer a deep breath.

Failure is really the one opportunity to plug in more intelligently.

Getting tired is the worst excuse. Get your butt in shape.

When your opponent is stretching, you're fetching.

Concentration is having the maintenance man blowing off the sidewalk and you didn't hear him.

You need to build a foundation. If not, the house falls down.

What you may see is different than what Rick Macci.

If you fail to prepare, you're preparing to fail.

If you do your home work, you have less work to do at home.

If you give 100 percent on every point, you're kidding yourself. You can do better.

If you get mad, you're getting better at getting mad.

If you don't run, you're better at not running.

If you stand, you get better at standing.

Show me a player with incredible balance and you're in the right sport.

It's OK to get knocked down. What happens next says it all.

When they are scurrying, you are hurrying.

A bad temper is a real key to failure.

Practice more than anybody in the world. Now that is dedication.

The ball is only as low as you make it. Bend.

Every day make today better than yesterday, if you can remember that today.

What is good? What is great? Good and great is compared to whom?

Show me a player who hits the big shot when it counts and I'll show you courage.

It's not how much you know. It's what you don't know and want to know.

If you dig deep you might find oil, but most of all you'll find success.

If you stay in the box, you can't think out of the box.

Believing is so, so powerful; so is doubt. Now you choose.

If you want to be a true champion, start changing your attitude today.

Calmness and intensity are the ultimate combination in competition.

Believing leads to achieving.

Tennis is a game. Games are fun! Enjoy the battle.

If you believe you will achieve.

You play with your skill, but you really win with your will.

If you always play nervous, just buy a ticket and watch.

Negative people get negative results.

A bad attitude is a real key to failure.

The mind is either for you or against you.

Little Steps = Big Results.

Sweat, Pain, Determination. That's a start.

Good is pretty good, greatness is the goal.

No fear - a big key to greatness.

Mental toughness is hitting three double faults in a row, then hitting an ace.

It's better to ask the coach a lot of questions than to have all the answers.

If you love, just love to compete, you're a real competitor.

If you think someone is unbeatable, they have just become even better.

If you don't love to run, please take up golf.

If your opponent's serve is really fast, slow it down in your mind.

All greatness has to come from you and you alone.

If you did a good job, that is a big difference than a great job.

If you stay after practice and hit serves, your mind gets better than your serve.

If you reach for the stars, you might as well become one also.

Always be ready, then you don't have to get ready.

A positive attitude is more positive than any stroke.

It's easy to be a pro. To make a great living as a pro, that's a different goal.

Believe and act. It is impossible to fail.

Flash sells tickets, substance wins matches.

The fences are out. Run.

If you ever want to play up to your ability, let it happen.

If your feet are always moving, you're in the right sport.

Anybody can come close. Closing on anybody is closure.

You might win the battle but lose the war. Think bigger.

I will never, never be broken down by anybody. Never ever.

Think Big. Be Big.

I have no doubt that I will reach my goal. No doubt.

If you refuse to accept anything but your best, you very often get it.

A true winner refuses to be denied. That is attitude.

Play the ball, don't let it play you.

If someone says you can't do it, it is so fulfilling to prove them wrong.

Attitude can and will determine altitude.

If you love to run, you'll run into greatness.

Just get the ball and keep your mouth shut.

The toughest game is the mind game. It is you against you. Good luck.

Excuses are OK if OK is the goal.

I like the inside out forehand. I like what is inside better.

If you hate to lose, I mean really hate to lose, now you're a real competitor.

It shows what you are really made of when you lose.

It is the quality of the consistency, not just being consistent.

Players who develop --- develop.

The mind is never neutral. It's either for you or against you.

Picture it in your mind before it happens.

Show me a player with unreal persistence. I'll show you a real competitor.

When you're so tired that you can't go any further, you may be in the round of 16.

A powerful serve is a real weapon, but the real weapon is your mind.

The best players have the best attitudes.

If you keep pushing the ball, you'll be a great 12-and-under player. Hit the ball.

If you play the ball, it doesn't matter who is across the net.

Fear is crippling, build courage and belief Monday through Sunday. No fear.

Life and tennis are like a boomerang. Things just come back at you.

Feel like you are in a bubble and before you know it the match is over.

Someday, somewhere, somebody will get your shot, so think bigger.

Players who say "I can't" see what they want to see.

It's mind over matter, if it matters to you how the mind works.

It's OK to follow the leader unless you want to be the leader.

Persistence is the real X factor.

Obstacles are those scary things you see when you take your eyes off your goals.

Don't wait…Go get it.

Winners expect to win in advance.

Goals are great to have, if great is the goal.

Being ready is being ready before you should be ready.

Show me a competitor who loves to compete on every point and I'll show you the definition of a competitor.

What you think of yourself is more important than what your opponent thinks.

If you want a lot of trophies you can buy them. The feeling of victory is the real trophy.

If every day you try to be better than the day before, you're better off than the day before.

If you reach for the SKY you can't reach it, but it's not out of reach.

Some people look at the exact same thing and see the exact opposite. See what I mean?

It isn't hard to figure out why things get harder if you are hard headed.

If you ever really accept losing don't enter, so you'll stay tied for last.

Tennis is like boxing, except you have a racquet instead of a glove, so be ready to move!

Pressure has to be your best friend. If it is, you'll deliver at crunch time.

Hit and react, it is spelled HITREACT.

Tennis is a game of time. It is either for you or against you.

If you're 100% ready to play, you'll play 100% ready.

If you're always negative, you get better at being negative.

If you keep getting mad, you get better at getting mad.

If you don't bend you get better at not bending.

If you don't adjust your feet, you get better at not adjusting.

There's an old saying, if you can't beat em, join em. I say don't join em, you should've been better prepared.

If you always think ahead you'll be ahead of the thinking.

Go meet it, greet it, beat it, defeat it.

The greatest thing since sliced bread in tennis is a great slice backhand angled short.

Even if you're on the right track, you could get hit by a train if you just sit there. Move!!!

Risky is good, risky is bad. You will know how much you can risk.

I love, just love, the word impossible. Break it up and it says, I'm possible!

Hope for the very best. Expect the very worst. If it happens you're ready!

Remember each day is like a Broadway play ... unrehearsed!

Have the courage to follow your heart. Your heart beats everything every second!

I just love to lay a rock solid foundation with the bricks others have thrown at me.

Age is a number. Dreams and goals outnumber age.

Losing is not failing. Failing is not trying.

Roll the dice, take chances, have courage and you will sometimes fail. But sadness and pain build courage!

The best way to deliver the goods is to get the goods to deliver! Sound good? Goodie!

Luck happens to everybody if you work hard. It is you playing you in life and in sports. Your opponents just participate.

Losing, pain, frustration will end. If you quit, that lasts forever.

If you're dialed in, you don't have to call 911.

Greatness feels the game is never ever over. They just ran out of time.

Getting tired is for quitters. Champions quit when they win.

Either you're all in or all out. That says it all about the ins and outs!

It takes real courage, I mean unreal courage, to push yourself to places you haven't been before. That place awaits great things.

Give me an athlete with determination and persistence and they never will fail. Ever!

No. 1. Remember last time I looked there was room at the top.

Once you make up your mind you can do something, you're 100 percent absolutely correct.

The road to greatness has no stop sign, just yield and caution.

People say success is a matter of luck. Ask a failure!

When you better your best your best has just gotten better.

Have a plan: Know where you're going. If not, trust me, everybody will tell you where to go!

Greatness can be achieved. Remember, nobody started out great and you don't have to be great to even start. Isn't that just great?!

Negative people feel they get no breaks. Wait til they have a compound fracture!

Go for your shots. Six-feet long is a heck of a lot better than six-feet under!!!

Many players get way too upset. By the way, if you stay positive, you can pull the upset!!!

Age is a number. Dreams and goals outnumber age.

Roll the dice, take chances, have courage. Sadness and pain build courage!

Luck happens to everybody if you work hard.

It is you playing you, period, in sports and life. Good luck!

It is OK to quit, and that is if you smoke!

Everybody wants to change the scene. You really need to change yourself.

If you think you can't, you're 100 percent right.

Accidents occur in the blink of an eye. So make sure you turn on your blinker.

Everybody uses remote control to change the channel. Only a few use self control to change the situation.

In poker, one of a kind is a tough hand. In life, one of a kind is a great hand.

Remember, even if you're on the right track you will get hit by a train if you just sit there. Move.

You're either all in or all out.

Consistency is the name of the game. Are you dialed in? If so call 1-800-CONSISTENCY.

Will defeats skill always.

Preparation is the key to everything, especially your car.

If you really fear something, do something you really fear to become more fearless.

If you dwell in the past, the grade you will get is an A in history!

I feel there are five types of happening people: 1. Those who watch things happen; 2. Those who make things happen; 3. Those who wish things would happen; 4. Those who felt things happened; 5. Those who wondered what the hell just happened.

14

DELIVERING THE GOODS / SPECIAL DELIVERY

Here is a smorgasbord of what is on the Macci menu when I'm delivering a message while I'm coaching:

If you set the table, you gotta eat! What I mean: Short ball, put it away.

Airmail: Go upstairs.

Check out the balcony: Lob.

Watch for the lobster: They are going to lob.

Pop the popcorn, extra butter: Move your feet!

Tap the dog: Palm down on the forehand.

You're in the neighborhood: You're in the game.

Be like Visa: Be everywhere.

Be like Allstate at the net: The good hands people.

Nudge your brother: Elbow back on the forehand.

Shake and bake: Move in and out of the baseline.

Turn the doorknob: Rotate forearm when creating topspin on the forehand.

Wax on / wax off Karate Kid Part 1: Rotate forearm / hand on forehand stroke.

Knife in knife out: Lead with edge in and out of back area when serving.

Prevent defense: Get back far by the fence and scrap.

Flow and go: Move through your approach shot.

When you're out of position don't be a magician: Play smart.

Come to the net like a German shepherd is chasing you: Run!

Time your split like an airplane landing: Move in and out and forward.

Roller derby: Angle.

More mustard: Hit it.

Turn down the volume: Relax.

Plug in: Wake up.

See you later: Put it away.

Good night: Game over.

Bye bye: Gone.

Lock it: Prepare early.

Mail it in: Automatic.

Take the temperature: Feel what is going on in the match.

Test the water: Try something different.

Keep it in the freezer: Build in hesitation of the serve.

Be like Domino's Pizza: You've got to deliver.

Knock knock: Wake up and answer the bell.

Set up shop: The match is going to last awhile.

Bingo: You win.

Refuel: Get water.

Juice it: Hit it.

One stop shopping: You need a complete game.

It's open like 7/11: All day, all night.

All day all night: All the time.

Like shock absorbers: Use your legs.

Sit in the chair: Bend.

Dip it. Flip it. Rip it: Mix it up.

Variety pack: Learn every shot.

Use the Vegematic: Slice and dice.

Snap crackle pop: Go after your serve.

The Maxwell coffee approach: A good effort to the last drop shot.

The Timex way: You'll take a licking but keep on ticking.

Visa and anticipation are similar: It's everywhere you want to be.

Be like Avis: Try harder.

Be like Nike: Just do it.

Bring you're A game like American Express: Don't leave home without it.

Hit like BMW: The ultimate driving machine.

Have half volley like Bounty: The quick picker upper.

Play the match like Burger King: Have it your way.

The Federal Express effort: When you absolutely, positively have to play into the night.

The John Deere approach: Move like a Deere.

Laser World: Hit lower.

Check out the third floor: Hit higher.

Ankle breaker: Hit behind them.

Work the pocket: Adjust your feet around the ball like a quarterback.

Slow death: Make 'em run.

Heavy duty: More spin.

Bacon and eggs/peanut butter and jelly: Put together combos like that.

The White House or the Outhouse: The best or the worst.

Gamer: You just love to compete.

Overcooked it: Hit too hard.

Fresh out of the oven: New balls.

You're over-baking it: Thinking too much.

Ninth inning: Last game.

Fourth quarter: Almost done.

The Kentucky Fried Chicken approach: Do one thing and do it well

The Taco Bell strategy: Think out of the box.

Train like Subway: Be fresh.

The Papa John's strategy: Better footwork, better strokes, better playing.

Toast: Done.

Be like Delta Airlines: Be ready before they are.

Move like Delta: Your opponent will love the way you fly.

Be like Jaguar: Born to perform.

Train like Citibank: Never sleep.

The Chevy approach: Be like a rock.

You like Frosted Flakes: You're grrrrrreeeaaaaat.

Pull the trigger: Go for it.

Reel it in: Don't over hit.

Massage it: Grab it and control it.

Gathering mode: Get under control prior to hitting.

Unplugged: Mentally not there.

Tighten the screws: Bear down.

If you add some mustard, you won't have to catsup.

Frozen rope: Tight spin.

24/7: All day.

See ya later: Put away shot.

Shape it: More arc.

Lock in: Bear down.

The Denny's approach: Your only Grand Slam ever.

The Michael Jackson forehand: Just beat it.

Grunt like Verizon: Can you hear me now?

A Kodak moment: Remember that picture.

Follow through like Reynolds: The best wrap around.

Take the Pringles footwork approach. Once you pop, you can't stop.

Dial it in: Don't over-hit.

Hammer time: Go for it.

Knife City: Go after your slice.

Freddy Krueger shot: Scary.

Hello: Wake up.

Bring your lunch: You're going to be here awhile.

Wanting the Baghdad approach: Shock and awe.

Road work: Putting in the hours.

Load and explode: Bend and fire.

Like a goalie: Nothing gets by you.

Facial: Hit at them when they are at the net.

Dot the eye: Stick the volley.

Call a cab: You gotta move.

Turbo booster: You need to get quicker.

Bring your hard hat: Be ready to work.

The appetizer: Easy first round.

Main course: Tough match.

The Tin Man: Loosen up.

The scarecrow: Tighten up.

The lion: Need more heart.

Stop and pop: Get set and fire.

Stones: Hard hands.

Donuts: 6-0 6-0.

Breadsticks: 6-1 6-1.

Gardening: Pick up the balls.

Nasty: Great.

Illegal: Great shot.

Throw the Hail Mary: Hit up/out on the serve.

Throw the ax: Lead with edge when serving.

High five a giant: Reach up and turn palm outward when serving.

Extra sauce: More power.

Batting practice: Keep swinging.

A Quiznos Day: Toasty.

Sherman Williams: Paint the lines.

Previews of coming of attractions: What it will be like in the pros.

Razor blade approach: Slow death.

Five-star: Great service.

Don't bow during your performance: You're bending at the waist. Bend after your performance.

Merry Christmas: You got a present.

Fourth of July: Going to be an argument.

Press the reset button: Start over.

Down goes Frazier: Knockout punch.

Thanksgiving approach: Carve him up.

TGIF: You're in the quarters.

Fasten your seat belt: Hold on.

15

MATCH POINT

Over my career, thousands of people in all walks of life -- whether it be the mom, the dad -- no matter what they do, many people have said, "Why don't you present your message on television? Why don't you commentate? The way you explain a tennis match or the way you analyze it and the way that you can hold an audience or connect the dots or the way you wire things together is so crystal clear."

They say it really brings the listener or the viewer in and they're very intrigued. Plus it's backed up by cutting edge biomechanics and unique sound knowledge of the game. I've created a situation where I'm fortunate that I teach so many people that there really hasn't been time for me to do TV. But I will delve into television a little bit, and it might not even be from a tennis point of view or commentating or analyzing a tennis match.

I think that because I am able to communicate with the public with a different way, with a different point of reference, with a different angle, and with the terminology that people can relate to with enthusiasm, makes me think that could be in the cards for me if I have time. I also know I want to do exactly what I'm doing now as long as I can do it. If you have a gift, you owe it to yourself to share that skill with others but TV does give you the ultimate platform.

I love helping others and the best thing I could do is give my knowledge and insight to millions of people, whether it be more public speaking or on television. It's just a matter of finding the time to do it and making it a priority, which is a good problem.

Tennis has given me that arena to do my thing and influence others. You acquire the knowledge as you go along, especially from a technical point of view. Remember, it's not what you know, even though that's huge, it's what you know and how you say it, why you say it, when you're going to say it, and who you're saying it to, because every day is a new day. Every person feels something different each day.

You've got to do what I call take the temperature and there's an art to that. There's a skill to doing that. That's one of the things I've been blessed with. I know how to maximize a person's ability on that day and I'm on a mission to do that. I want that day to extract greatness -- more from me and even more from them.

When it's all said and done, I don't have guarantees, nobody does. It really takes two to tango, and when you have any success, there's a lot of luck involved. You can't win the Kentucky Derby unless you have a thoroughbred. But it is also not by accident that there have been so many kids win nationals or junior Grand Slam tournaments or kids who went on to have a lot of success in the pros. There were a lot of dots that needed to be connected, a lot of seeds planted, watered and cultivated. There was a lot of rewiring of kids' mindset. Parents too even though some short circuited! Ha!

There's a big difference between having someone become very good or great and there's a big difference between someone becoming good and kind of good. I think all these things have to meet at a certain point and it's all timing. And then it's what you do with that backdrop.

What I like to think of more than anything is: Whatever I've got to do today is all that really matters. I've always been able to focus on what's ahead of me and make that the most important thing with my heart and soul. I think any person who you're teaching, no matter what age, can feel that. They feel that passion. They feel that you're in there.

I think that is huge, the influence you can have on young people to get them to jump higher, run faster and be more dedicated and do a little bit more. The power that you have is incredible. I think that's one of the gifts that I've always had, when you're out there helping anybody, any age, no matter what level. They don't have to be nationally ranked. They can be a five-year-old. I know if I did an amazing job because that's what I expect of myself. That's what people have to understand. It's what you expect of yourself each day that determines everything. I expect to be better every day. You've got to keep improving, Don't look back. Reach higher. Expect more and you know what? You will improve because you didn't look back and you expected more and now you've reached greater heights.

In life, one of the things we have is a choice. Everything is a choice. No choice is sometimes a very good choice. Even though the weather dictates things and people dictate things and situations dictate things, within that realm you still have a choice. In everything that is happening, you're making choices every day -- to be happy or sad, to do this or do that, to talk louder or softer, go here, go there. You have a choice and as long as you keep trying to be the best you can be and get better each day, good things are going to happen. This is how greatness frames up life, almost a game within a game.

When you sit around and wait for things to happen, they're not going to fall into your lap. It's not going to be. Make it fall into your lap. When you're doing the best, you can look in the mirror because the mirror test always says it all. It says whose fault it is and who should get the credit. When you can look in the mirror and say, "I did the best I could," that's what it's all about. No more discussion.

You can't always control the situation, OK? But you can influence it. That's why I know in my career I've tried to do the best I could for each student, and that's all that matters. If you can honestly look at yourself and say that, great -- and I can do this 100 percent. I really can. I was all in every day. No short cuts. All in, 24/7.

To have even that type of attitude you've got to love what you do and you have to have a passion. I get up in the morning at 4 or 5, which I have for the last 25 years. For a lot of people, the first step out of bed is always tough, but once you make the first step you have to have a purpose. Just like in any sport the first step is the most important step. The minute the water hits my face and my eyes are awake I'm ready to go like no tomorrow. And that's from someone who's teaching 60 hours a week of lessons and doing this a long time. If you love something and have passion for it, greatness is the main course on the menu.

I have just as much energy and drive today as when I first started. That's because what I expect of myself and people can feel that. But most of all, I've got passion. I expect to improve every day. Period. And I hear people can feel that. I expect the student to do the same also. We both do and will.

That's why I feel like some of this can flow into commentating and other things about the way that I can explain it, of my experience being in the trenches. I've been in the trenches just as much if not more than anybody who has taught the game of tennis, simply because I've done so much one-on-one stuff over the past 30 years. I've seen it from so many directions and I've always wanted to get better, I've always wanted to improve, I've always wanted to know more. Life changes and the game of tennis has changed. It is much different than when I taught junior phenom Tommy Ho when this whole thing started in the late 1980s. I don't teach anything like I did then, especially understanding biomechanically how the body works. But I always knew how the strongest, most powerful part of your body worked and that was your brain. That to me has been a life and game changer. But my Greenville, Ohio, wires are the same. They are just a new and improved wiring. Some now in 3D!

I think the same. I speak a lot the same. I can still see things the way I see things, but the game has changed. If you're going to be a teacher or a role model, or if you're going to try to influence other people, you have an obligation to the public to be the best you can be and continue your education, if you want to. If you don't want to, that's fine, but this is what has worked for me.

Even today when I watch other sports on TV I can almost analyze why somebody dropped a ball or why somebody misses a shot, whether it's their footwork or they choke or there's a technical flaw or it's a blend or a combination of a couple things. I can remember watching Jennifer when she was on the pro tour and I'd be sitting at home with someone and I'd say, "Cross court, cross court, down the line, short angle." Before she'd even hit the ball I could tell where she'd hit it. And I can pretty much do that with the Williams sisters. That's not just because I know their game that well, which is obvious, it's just that when you've done this for so long and the tennis court has been your living room for 30 years and you're on it, you know every piece of clay court or hard court there is, and you just see it so much differently. It is kind of scary. I like scary. Boo!!!

But more importantly, I've always had that ability, even as a kid, to see a lot of things and look right through things and analyze things. You take that wiring and the dedication to do what I've done and it's been very rewarding. When it's all said and done you keep the blinders on. I'm just one of the guys. My main responsibility is who I'm going to teach today. And that's it. It's not what I've done in the past. And that's a problem with a lot of people. They accomplish good things or they win something and they think they've done it all. I've never been like that.

Everybody wants credit and acknowledgment and stuff like that. That's probably why I've waited so long to write a book. People have been telling me to write a book for 20 years. People wanted me to do TV for 20 years. And I just kept building the blocks higher and bigger and better. Then you turn around and you look, wow, what I built is pretty solid. But today I have one concern and one concern only: I've got to do better today than I did yesterday. And I hope you do the same thing.

To do anything great, as I said, it starts with passion. Passion conquers everything. It makes you more determined, more focused, and you handle things easier with this inner drive. My "Maccisms" are just some nuggets of what I expect, what I believe and how I look at life. Whether it's right or wrong, good or bad, I don't know, but it works for me and it helped me go from a sport I loved to play 24/7 to a sport I love to coach and rise to the top of the profession.

A few key staples you need that are very common to go from good to great are sprinkled by the self discipline you deliver day in and day out. Self control is huge. Managing your mood is a game changer with others. Also, putting your mind to work before your mouth opens is big time. Having the ability to ignore some things is a gift everybody should master. Being organized and dialed in on a regular basis creates an expectation of yourself and you become machine like. You make the most of your time. These qualities I feel serve as huge building blocks for greatness.

FULL CIRCLE

The tennis courts in Greenville, Ohio, that I played on, lived on, slept on, where it all started at age 13, at the time of this printing are being considered to be named the Rick Macci Tennis Courts! Wow! When I used to write my name in chalk on the court in the late 1960s and '70s as Rick Macci's Court, I guess the cold freezing Midwest winters and blistering summer heat has worn off my name, but it could be replaced with a monument! I guess you can only say one thing: Chalk it up to Macci magic! ☺

ALSO FROM
NEW CHAPTER PRESS

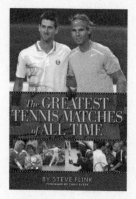

The Greatest Tennis Matches of All Time
By Steve Flink

Author and tennis historian Steve Flink profiles and ranks the greatest tennis matches in the history of the sport. Roger Federer, Billie Jean King, Rafael Nadal, Bjorn Borg, John McEnroe, Martina Navratilova, Rod Laver, Don Budge and Chris Evert are all featured in this book that breaks down, analyzes, and puts into historical context the most memorable matches ever played.

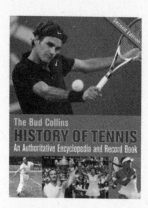

The Bud Collins History of Tennis
By Bud Collins

Compiled by the most famous tennis journalist and historian in the world, this book is the ultimate compilation of historical tennis information, including year-by-year recaps of every tennis season, biographical sketches of every major tennis personality, as well as stats, records, and championship rolls for all the major events.

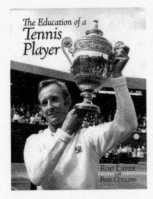

The Education of a Tennis Player

By Rod Laver with Bud Collins

Depicting the monumental achievements of a world-class athlete, this firsthand account documents Rod Laver's historic 1969 Grand Slam sweep of all four major tennis titles. This frank memoir details Laver's childhood, early career, and his most important matches. Each chapter also contains a companion tennis lesson, providing tips on how players of all levels can improve their own game and sharing strategies that garnered unparalleled success on the courts. Fully updated on the 40th anniversary of the author's most prominent triumph, this revised edition contains brand new content, including the story of Laver's courageous recovery from a near-fatal stroke in 1998.

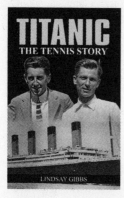

TITANIC: The Tennis Story
By Lindsay Gibbs

A stirring and remarkable story, this novel tells the tale of the intertwined life of Dick Williams and Karl Behr who survived the sinking of the *Titanic* and went on to have Hall of Fame tennis careers. Two years before they faced each other in the quarterfinals of the U.S. Nationals – the modern-day U.S. Open - the two men boarded the infamous ship as strangers. Dick, shy and gangly, was moving to America to pursue a tennis career and attend Harvard. Karl, a dashing tennis veteran, was chasing after Helen, the love of his life. The two men remarkably survived the sinking of the great vessel and met aboard the rescue ship *Carpathia*. But as they reached the shores of the United States, both men did all they could to distance themselves from the disaster. An emotional and touching work, this novel brings one of the most extraordinary sports stories to life in literary form. This real-life account – with an ending seemingly plucked out of a Hollywood screenplay - weaves the themes of love, tragedy, history, sport and perseverance.

www.NewChapterMedia.com